ORIGAMI
MYTHS & LEGENDS

Duy Nguyen

Sterling Publishing Co., Inc.
New York

Design by Judy Morgan
Edited by Claire Bazinet

Library of Congress Cataloging-in-Publication Data

Nguyen, Duy, 1960-
  Origami myths & legends / Duy Nguyen.
    p. cm.
  Includes index.
  ISBN 1-4027-1550-1
  1. Origami. I. Title: Origami myths and legends. II. Title.

TT870.N4873 2004
736'.982--dc22
                                    2004021537

10 9 8 7 6 5 4 3 2 1

Published by Sterling Publishing Co., Inc.
387 Park Avenue South, New York, NY 10016
© 2005 by Duy Nguyen
Distributed in Canada by Sterling Publishing
℅ Canadian Manda Group, 165 Dufferin Street
Toronto, Ontario, Canada M6K 3H6
Distributed in Great Britain and Europe by Chris Lloyd at Orca Book
Services, Stanley House, Fleets Lane, Poole BH15 3AJ, England
Distributed in Australia by Capricorn Link (Australia) Pty. Ltd.
P.O. Box 704, Windsor, NSW 2756, Australia

Printed in China

Sterling ISBN 1-4027-1550-1

Contents

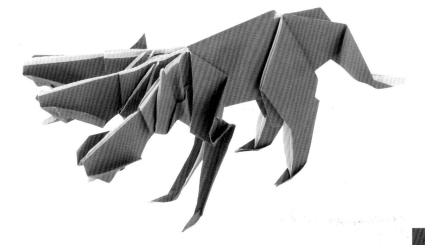

Preface

Some years ago, when I first began learning origami, I struggled with even the simplest folds. I would look back at the instructions given at the beginning of the book again and again, reviewing the basic folds. I also looked ahead, at the diagram showing the next step of whatever project I was folding, to see how it *should* look, to be certain I was following the instructions correctly. Looking ahead at the "next step," the result of a fold, is incidentally a very good way for a beginner to learn origami.

You will easily pick up this and other learning techniques as you follow the step-by-step directions given for this new collection, this time of creatures from myth and legend. Some are fairly easy to fold, formed from only a single square of paper. Others of these fabulous creatures may call for a good deal more time and effort, with smaller and tighter folds to add creative detail. But if you persevere, I guarantee the result will most certainly be worth it.

Duy Nguyen

Basic Instructions

Paper: Paper used in traditional origami is thin, keeps a crease well, and folds flat. Packets of specially designed sheets, about 6 and 8 inches square (15 and 21 cm), are available in various colors. A few of the projects given here call for a rectangular size or longer piece of paper, but this shouldn't be a problem. You can use plain white, solid-color, or even wrapping paper with a design only on one side and cut to size. Be aware, though, that some papers stretch slightly in length or width, which can cause folding problems, while others tear easily.

Beginners, or those concerned about getting their fingers to work tight folds, might consider using larger paper sizes. Regular paper may be too heavy to allow the many tight folds needed in creating more traditional, origami figures, with many folds, but fine for larger versions of these intriguing projects. So sit down, select some paper, and begin to fold and enjoy the wonderful art that is origami.

Glue: Use an easy-flowing but not loose paper glue. Use it sparingly; don't soak the paper. A flat toothpick makes a good applicator. Be sure to allow the glued form time to dry. Avoid stick glue, which can become overly dry and crease or damage your figure.

Technique: Fold with care. Position the paper, especially at corners, precisely and line edges up before creasing. Once you are sure of the fold, use a fingernail to make a clean, flat crease.

For more complex folds, create "construction lines." Fold and unfold, using simple mountain and valley folds, to pre-crease. This creates guidelines, and the finished fold is more likely to match the one shown in the book. Folds that look different, because the angles are slightly different, can throw you off. Don't get discouraged with your first efforts. In time, what your mind can create, your fingers can fashion.

Symbols & Lines

| Fold lines | valley | | Fold then unfold | |
| | mountain | | | |

Cut line

Pleat fold
(repeated folding)

Turn over or rotate

Crease line

Squaring-Off Paper

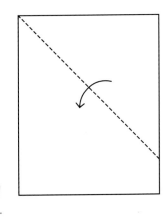

1

Take a rectangular sheet
of paper and valley fold it
diagonally to opposite edge.

2

Cut off excess on long side
as shown.

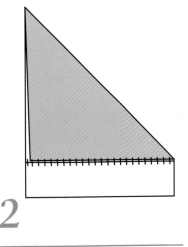

3

Unfold, and sheet is square.

Basic Folds

Kite Fold

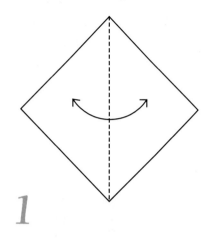

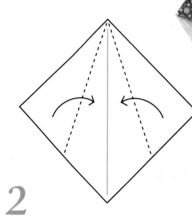

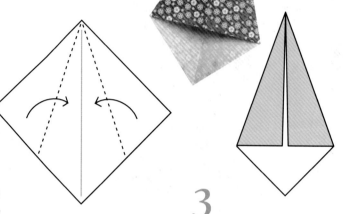

1
Fold and unfold a square diagonally, making a center crease.

2
Fold both sides in to the center crease.

3
This is a kite form.

Valley Fold   - - - - - - - - - - - - - - - - -

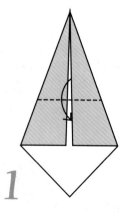

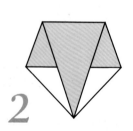

1
Here, using the kite, fold form toward you (forwards), making a "valley."

2
This fold forward is a valley fold.

Mountain Fold   - · - · - · - · - · - · -

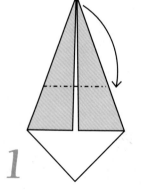

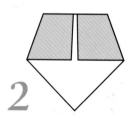

1
Here, using the kite, fold form away from you (backwards), making a "mountain."

2
This fold backwards is a mountain fold.

Inside Reverse Fold

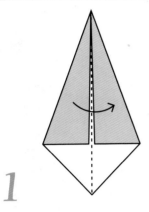

1
Starting here with a kite, valley fold kite closed.

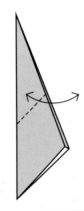

2
Valley fold as marked to crease, then unfold.

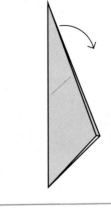

3
Pull tip in direction of arrow.

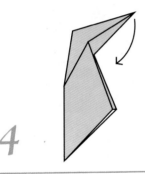

4
Appearance before completion.

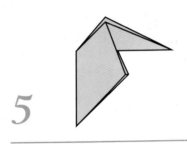

5
You've made an inside reverse fold.

Outside Reverse Fold

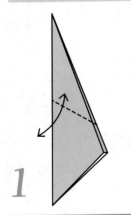

1
Using closed kite, valley fold, unfold.

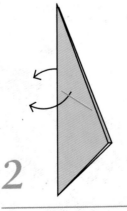

2
Fold inside out, as shown by arrows.

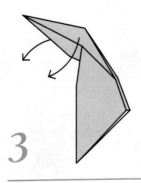

3
Appearance before completion.

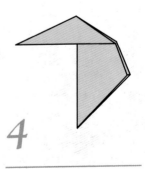

4
You've made an outside reverse fold.

Pleat Fold

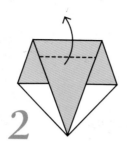

1

Here, using the kite, valley fold.

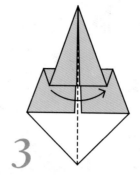

2

Valley fold back again.

3

This is a pleat. Valley fold in half.

4

You've made a pleat fold.

Pleat Fold Reverse

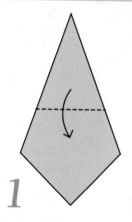

1

Here, using the kite form backwards, valley fold.

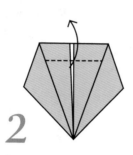

2

Valley fold back again for pleat.

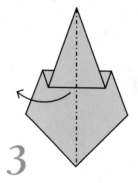

3

Mountain fold form in half.

4

This is a pleat fold reverse.

Squash Fold I

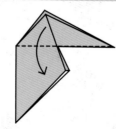

1

Using inside reverse, valley fold one side.

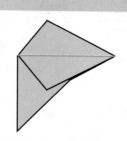

2

This is a squash fold I.

Squash Fold II

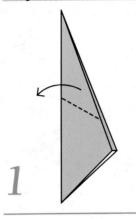 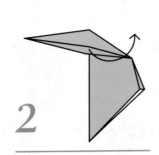  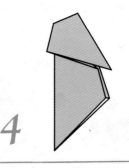

1
Using closed kite form, valley fold.

2
Open in direction of the arrow.

3
Appearance before completion.

4
You've made a squash fold II.

Inside Crimp Fold

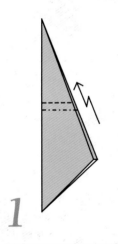 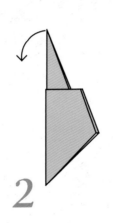

1
Here, using closed kite form, pleat fold.

2
Pull tip in direction of the arrow.

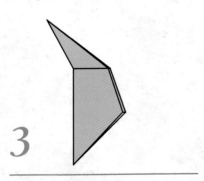

3
This is an inside crimp fold.

Outside Crimp Fold

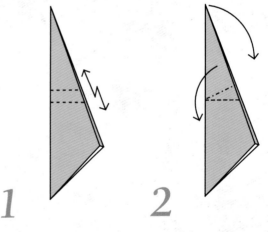

1
Here, using closed kite form, pleat fold and unfold.

2
Fold mountain and valley as shown, both sides.

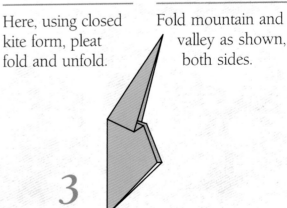

3
This is an outside crimp fold.

Basic Folds

Base Folds

Base folds are basic forms that do not in themselves produce origami, but serve as a basis, or jumping-off point, for a number of creative origami figures—some quite complex. As when beginning other crafts, learning to fold these base folds is not the most exciting part of origami. They are, however, easy to do, and will help you with your technique. They also quickly become rote, so much so that you can do many using different-colored papers while you are watching television or your mind is elsewhere. With completed base folds handy, if you want to quickly work up a form or are suddenly inspired with an idea for an original, unique figure, you can select an appropriate base fold and swiftly bring a new creation to life.

Base Fold I

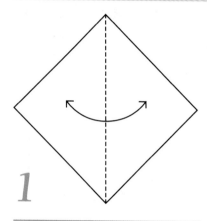

1

Fold and unfold in direction of arrow.

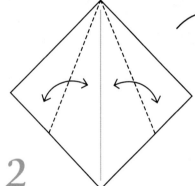

2

Fold both sides in to center crease, then unfold. Rotate.

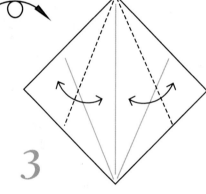

3

Fold both sides in to center crease, then unfold.

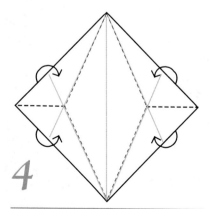

4

Pinch corners of square together and fold inward.

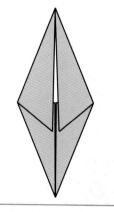

5

Completed Base Fold I.

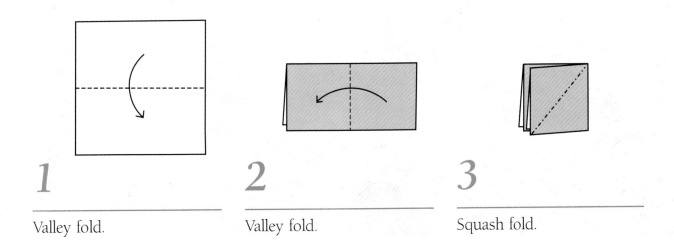

1
Valley fold.

2
Valley fold.

3
Squash fold.

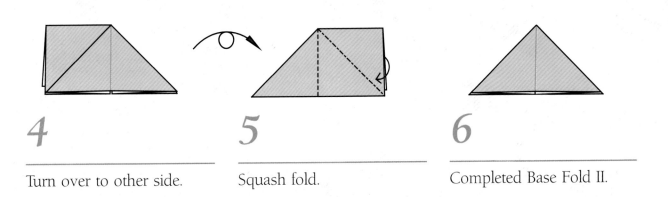

4
Turn over to other side.

5
Squash fold.

6
Completed Base Fold II.

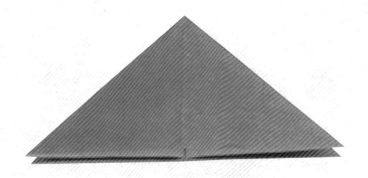

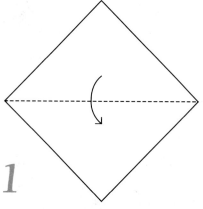

1

Valley fold.

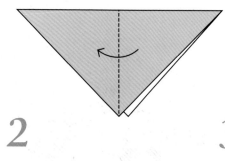

2

Valley fold.

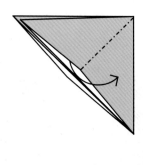

3

Squash fold.

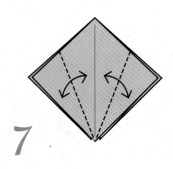

4

Turn over.

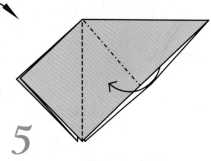

5

Squash fold.

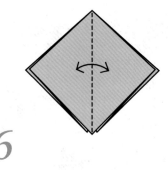

6

Valley fold, unfold.

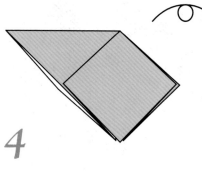

7

Valley folds, unfold.

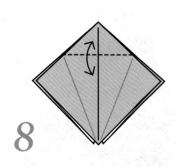

8

Valley fold, unfold.

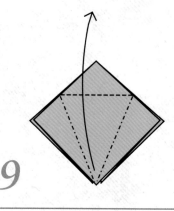

9

Pull in direction of arrow,
folding inward at sides.

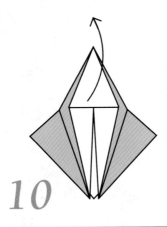

10

Appearance before completion of fold.

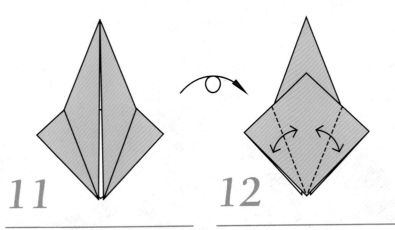

11

Fold completed. Turn over.

12

Valley folds, unfold.

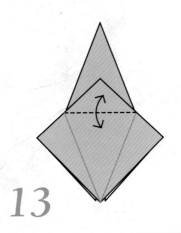

13

Valley fold, unfold.

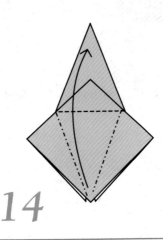

14

Repeat, again pulling in direction of arrow.

15

Appearance before completion.

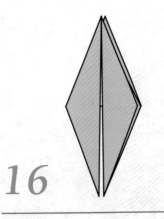

16

Completed Base Fold III.

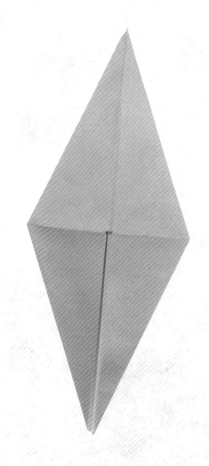

1

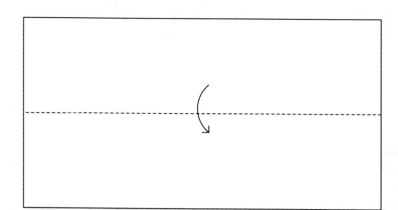

Valley fold rectangular paper (size variable) in half as shown.

2

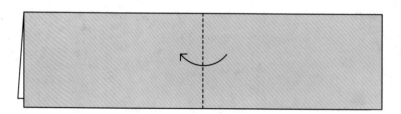

Valley fold in direction of arrow.

3

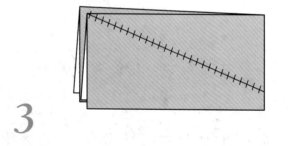

Make cut as shown.

4

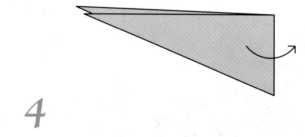

Unfold.

5

Unfold.

6

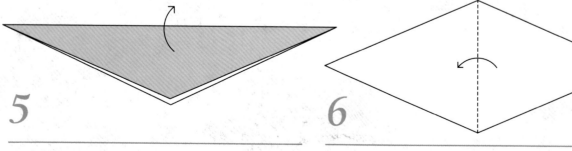

Valley fold in half.

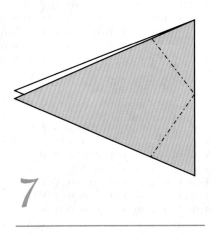

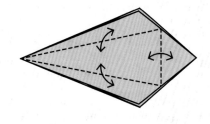

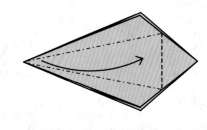

7

Inside reverse folds to inner center crease.

8

Valley fold and unfold to crease.

9

Pull in direction of arrow, and fold.

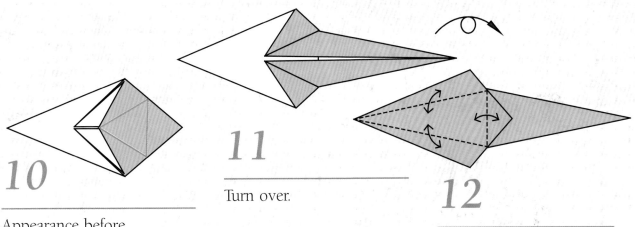

10

Appearance before completion.

11

Turn over.

12

Valley fold then unfold.

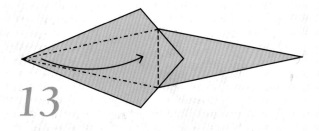

13

Again, pull in direction of arrow, and fold.

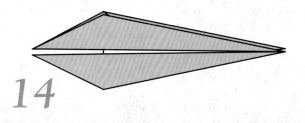

14

Completed Base Fold IV.

Flying Dragon

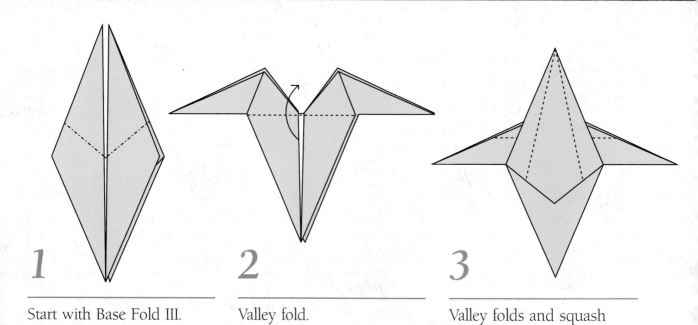

1

Start with Base Fold III.
Inside reverse folds.

2

Valley fold.

3

Valley folds and squash
folds.

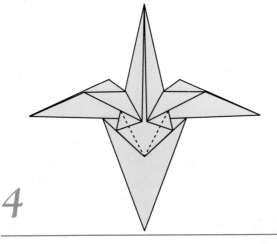

4

Valley folds.

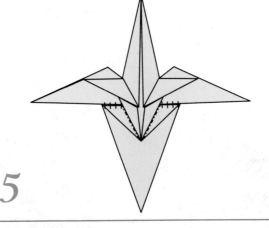

5

Make cuts, then mountain fold.

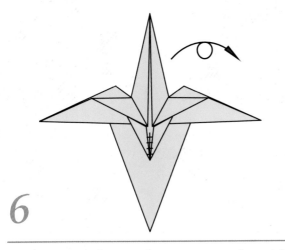

6

Cut point as shown, then turn to other side.

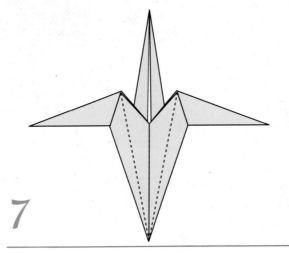

7

Valley folds.

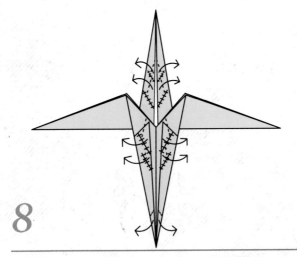

8

Make all cuts to front layer as shown here, then valley fold cut parts.

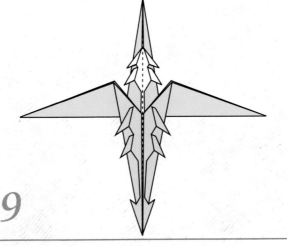

9

Valley fold in half.

Flying Dragon

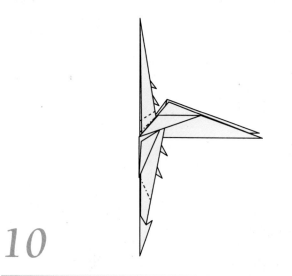

10

Crimp fold, and inside reverse fold.

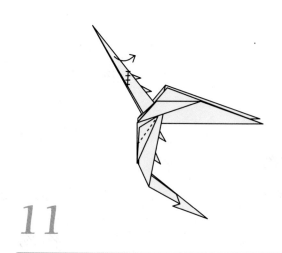

11

Cut and valley unfold. Outside reverse folds.

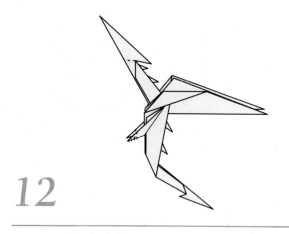

12

Cuts on both folds, then valley to sides.

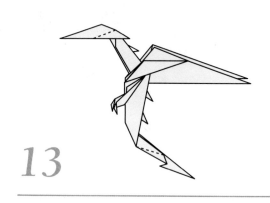

13

Valley folds.

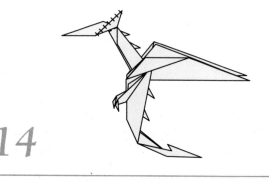

14

Cuts and valley folds.

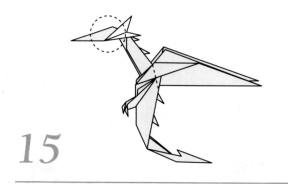

15

Valley folds both sides, then see close-up views for next steps.

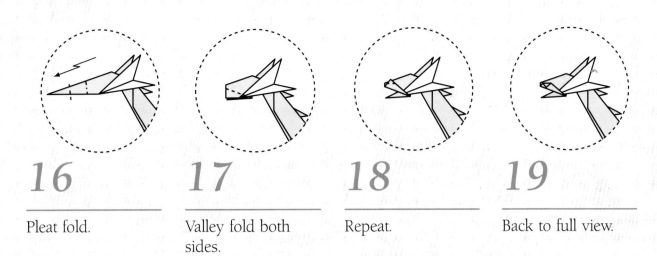

16
Pleat fold.

17
Valley fold both sides.

18
Repeat.

19
Back to full view.

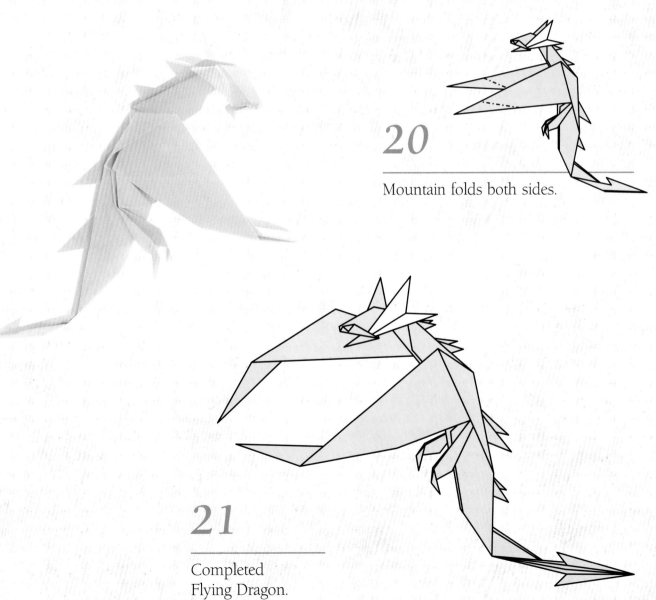

20
Mountain folds both sides.

21
Completed Flying Dragon.

Cyclops

1 Start with Base Fold III. Valley fold front and back.

2 Cut as shown, top flap only.

3 Valley folds.

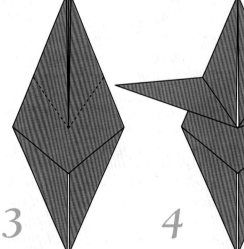

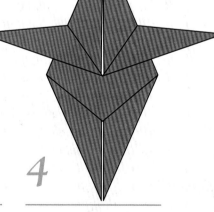

4 Turn over to other side.

20

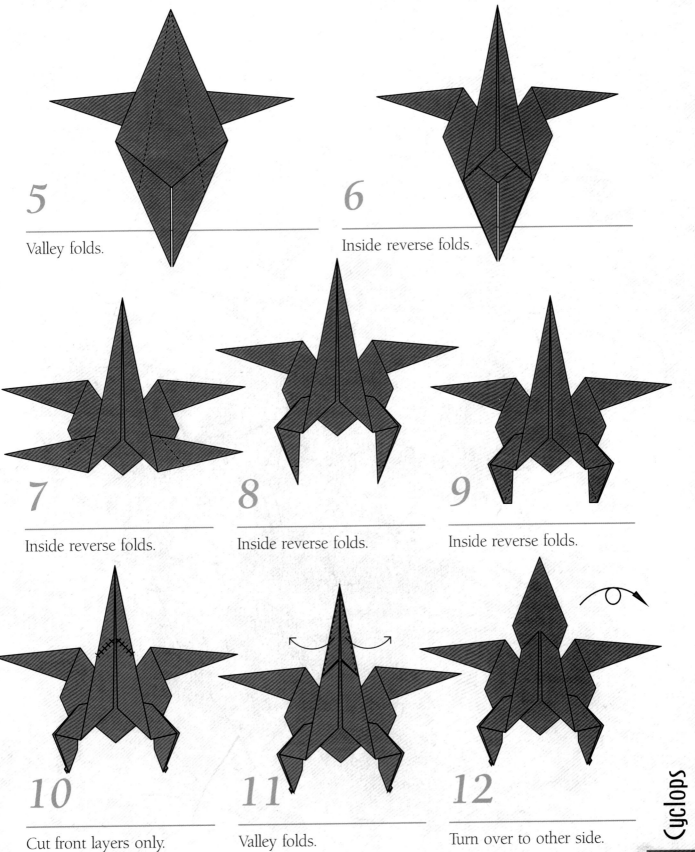

5

Valley folds.

6

Inside reverse folds.

7

Inside reverse folds.

8

Inside reverse folds.

9

Inside reverse folds.

10

Cut front layers only.

11

Valley folds.

12

Turn over to other side.

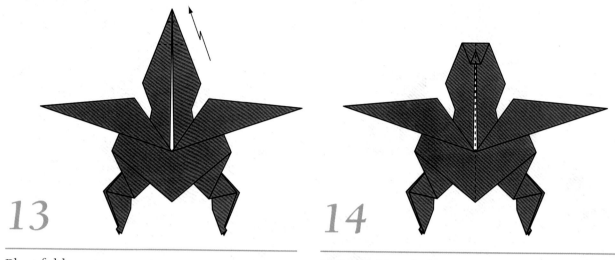

13

Pleat fold.

14

Valley fold in half.

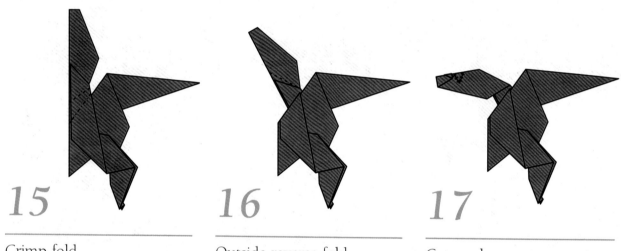

15

Crimp fold.

16

Outside reverse fold.

17

Cut as shown.

18

Valley and squash folds.

19

Inside reverse folds.

20

Outside reverse folds, both sides.

21

Crimp fold.

22

Outside reverse folds.

23

Inside reverse folds.

24

Outside reverse folds.

25

Completed Cyclops.

Cerberus

Part 1

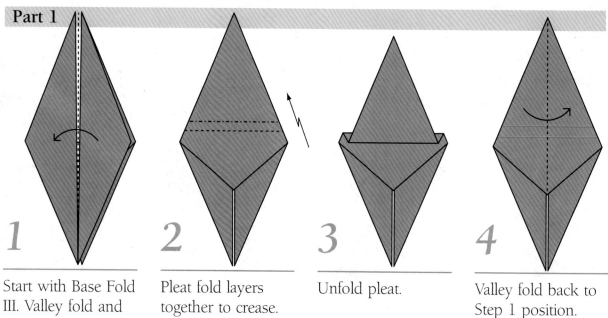

1 Start with Base Fold III. Valley fold and repeat behind.

2 Pleat fold layers together to crease.

3 Unfold pleat.

4 Valley fold back to Step 1 position.

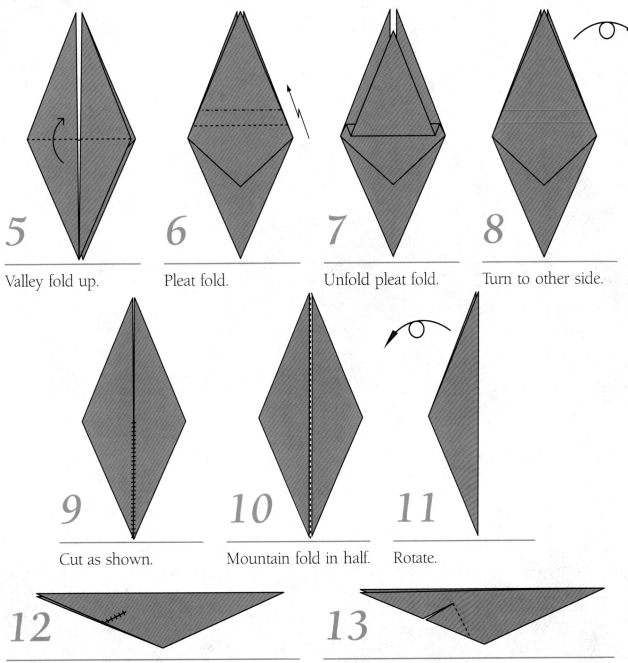

5

Valley fold up.

6

Pleat fold.

7

Unfold pleat fold.

8

Turn to other side.

9

Cut as shown.

10

Mountain fold in half.

11

Rotate.

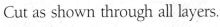

12

Cut as shown through all layers.

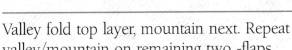

13

Valley fold top layer, mountain next. Repeat valley/mountain on remaining two -flaps.

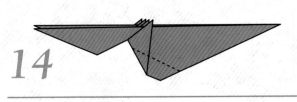

14

Valley/mountain fold inner layers as shown.

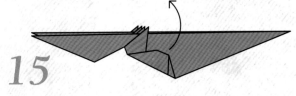

15

Valley unfold in direction of arrow.

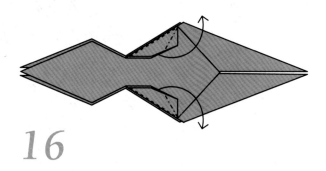

16

Squash folds.

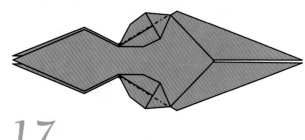

17

Mountain folds.

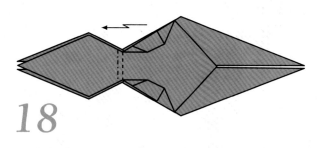

18

Pleat fold top layer.

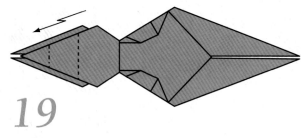

19

Pleat fold.

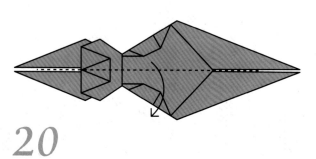

20

Valley fold top layer.

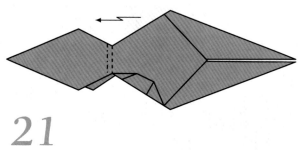

21

Pleat fold top layer.

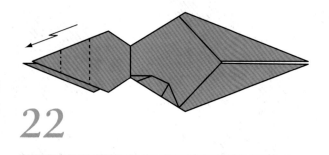

22

Pleat fold.

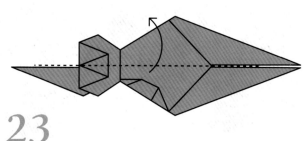

23

Valley fold.

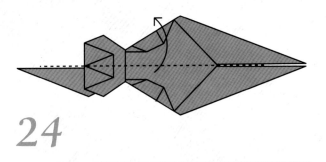

24

Valley fold.

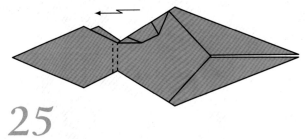

25

Pleat fold.

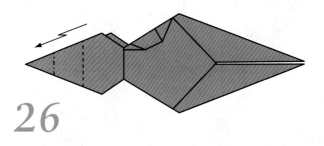

26

Pleat fold.

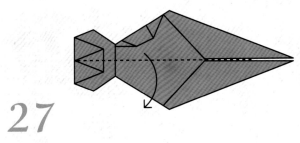

27

Valley fold.

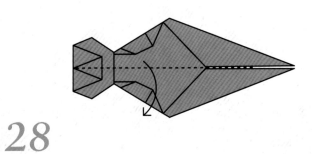

28

Valley fold in half.

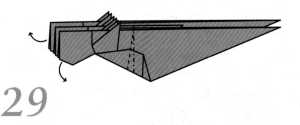

29

Open side layers and crimp all.

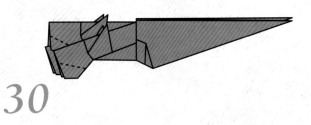

30

Valley fold front and back of each layer.

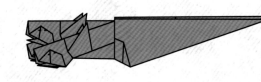

31

Valley fold all sides.

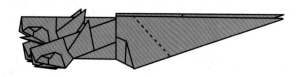
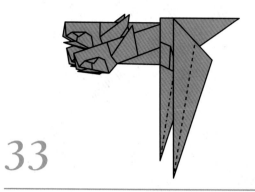

32

Valley fold front and back.

33

Valley fold both sides.

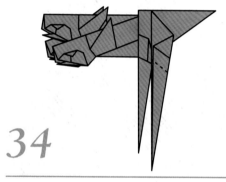
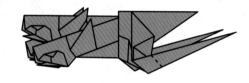

34

Outside reverse folds.

35

Outside reverse folds.

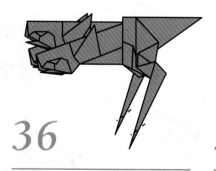
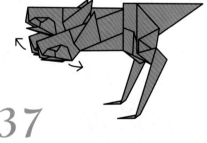

36

Inside reverse folds.

37

Separate heads to sides.

38

Completed part 1 of Cerberus.

1

Start with Base Fold III. Valley fold.

2

Turn over to other side.

3

Valley fold.

4

Valley folds.

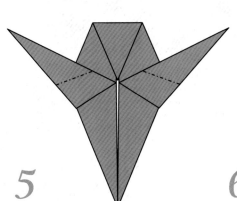

5

Inside reverse folds.

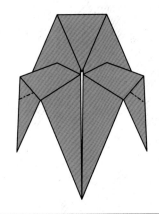

6

Inside reverse folds.

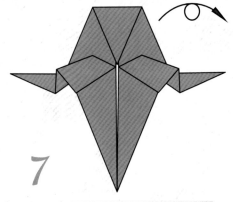

7

Turn over to other side.

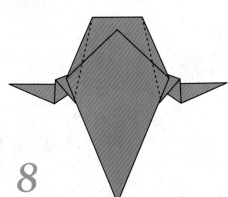

8

Valley folds.

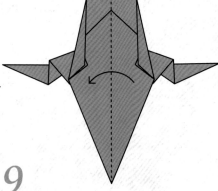

9

Valley fold in half.

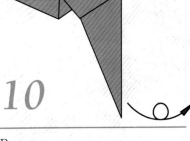

10

Rotate.

Cerberus

29

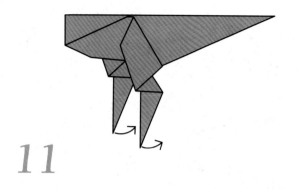

11

Pull and squash into position.

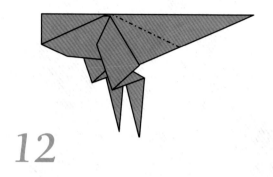

12

Inside reverse fold.

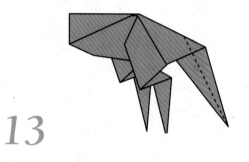

13

Valley folds.

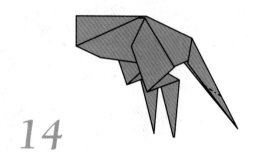

14

Inside reverse fold.

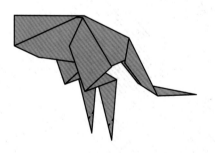

15

Outside reverse folds.

16

Complete part 2 of Cerberus.

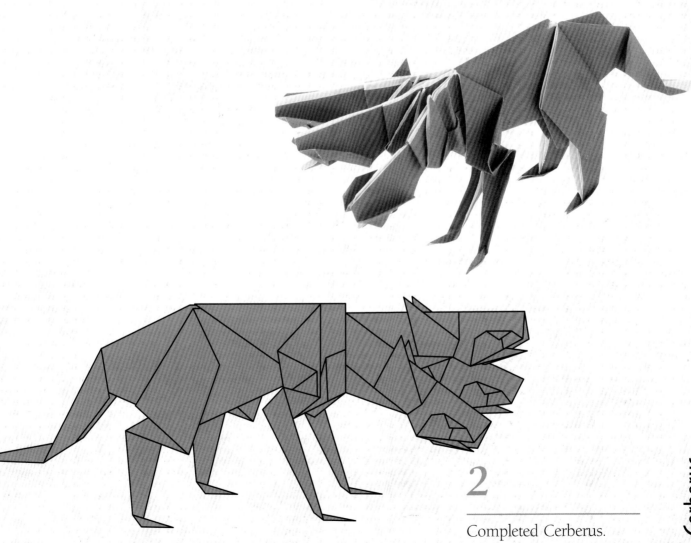

1

Join both parts together as shown and apply glue to hold.

2

Completed Cerberus.

Mermaid

Part 1

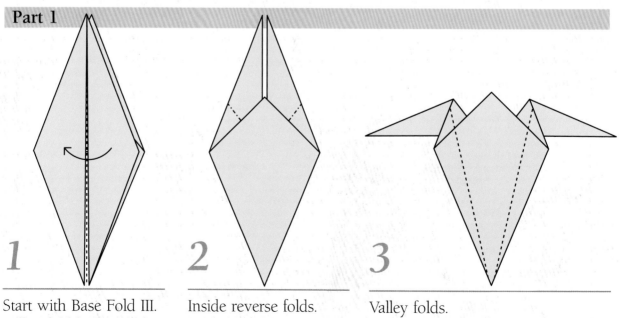

1
Start with Base Fold III.
Valley fold both sides.

2
Inside reverse folds.

3
Valley folds.

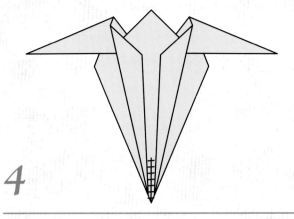

4

Make cut as shown.

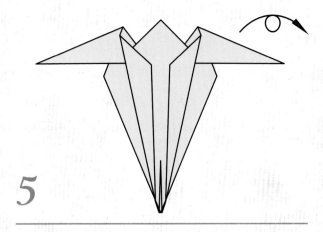

5

Turn over to other side.

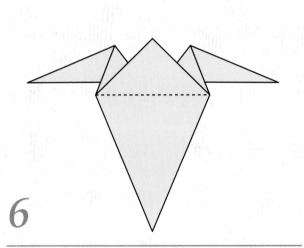

6

Valley fold.

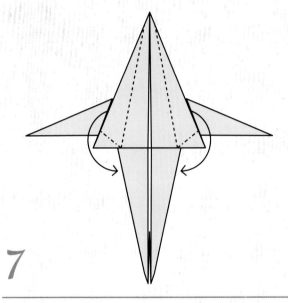

7

Valley and squash folds at same time.

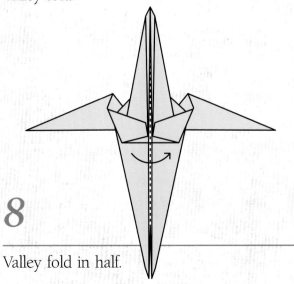

8

Valley fold in half.

9

Valley fold.

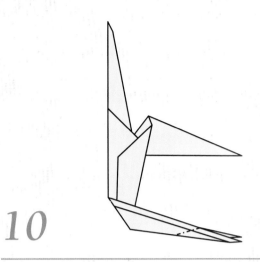

10

Mountain fold.

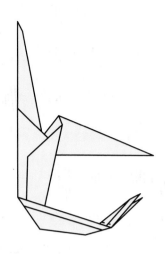

11

Valley fold.

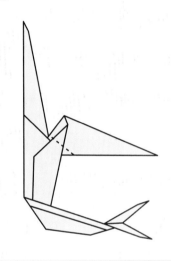

12

Valley fold both sides.

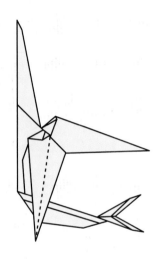

13

Valley fold.

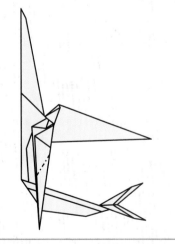

14

Inside reverse fold.

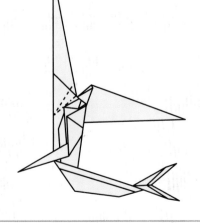

15

Crimp fold.

16

Outside reverse fold.

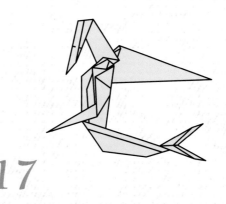

17

Outside reverse fold.

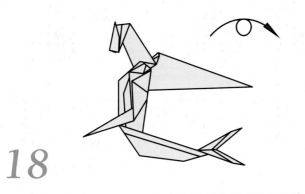

18

Turn over to other side.

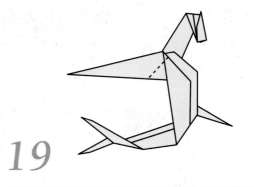

19

Valley fold.

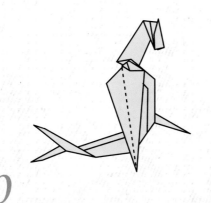

20

Valley fold.

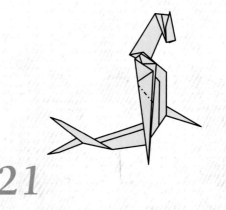

21

Inside reverse fold.

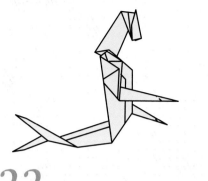

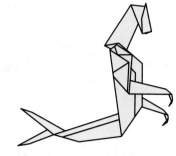

22

Inside reverse folds.

23

Outside reverse folds.

24

Completed part 1 of mermaid.

Part 2

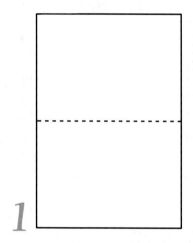

1

Valley fold 3" by 5" (8 by 13 cm) sheet.

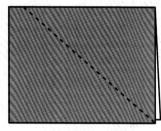

2

Inside reverse fold.

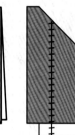

3

Cut as shown.

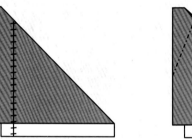

4

Mountain folds.

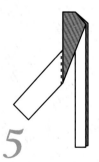

5

Valley folds.

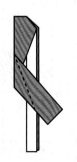

6

Valley folds.

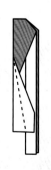

7

Valley folds.

8

Mountain folds.

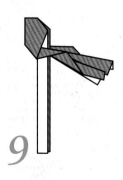

9

Completed part 2 of mermaid.

Mermaid

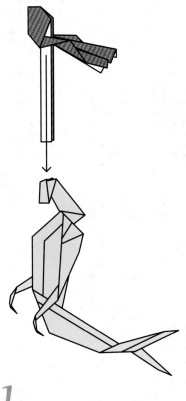

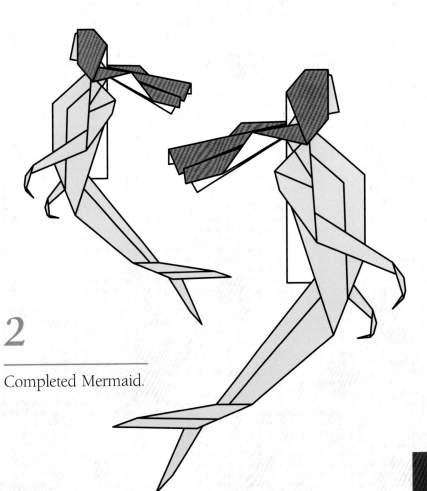

1

Join both parts together as shown and apply glue to hold. Trim excess if desired.

2

Completed Mermaid.

Unicorn

Part 1

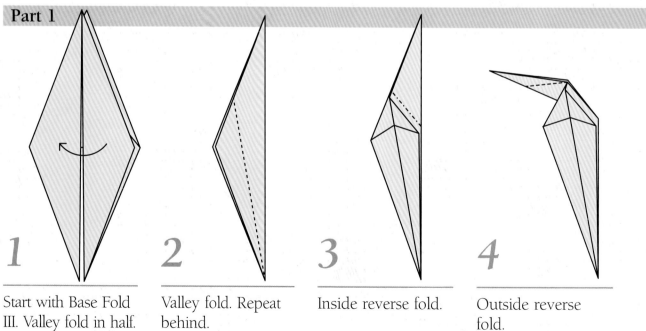

1
Start with Base Fold III. Valley fold in half.

2
Valley fold. Repeat behind.

3
Inside reverse fold.

4
Outside reverse fold.

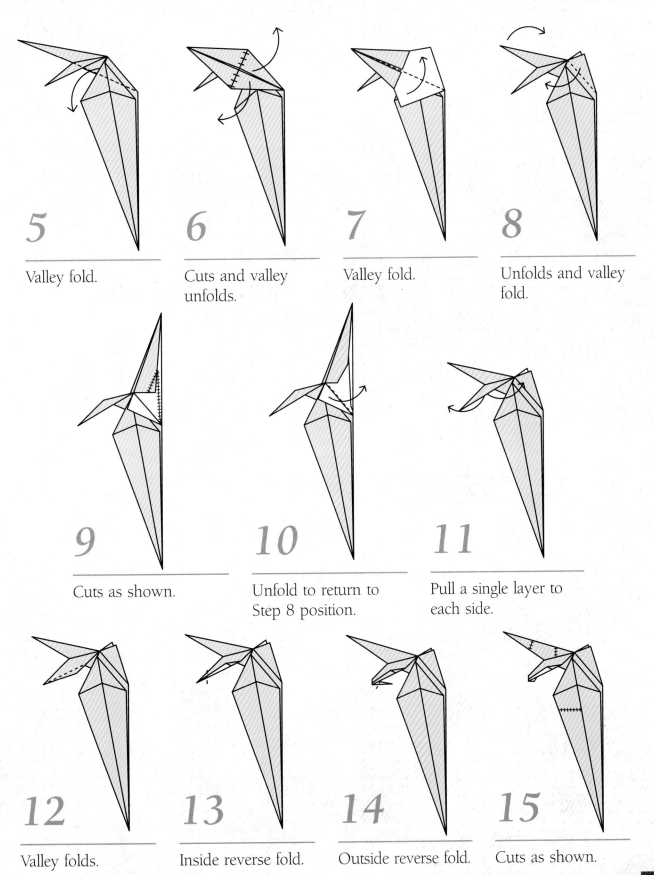

5

Valley fold.

6

Cuts and valley unfolds.

7

Valley fold.

8

Unfolds and valley fold.

9

Cuts as shown.

10

Unfold to return to Step 8 position.

11

Pull a single layer to each side.

12

Valley folds.

13

Inside reverse fold.

14

Outside reverse fold.

15

Cuts as shown.

Unicorn

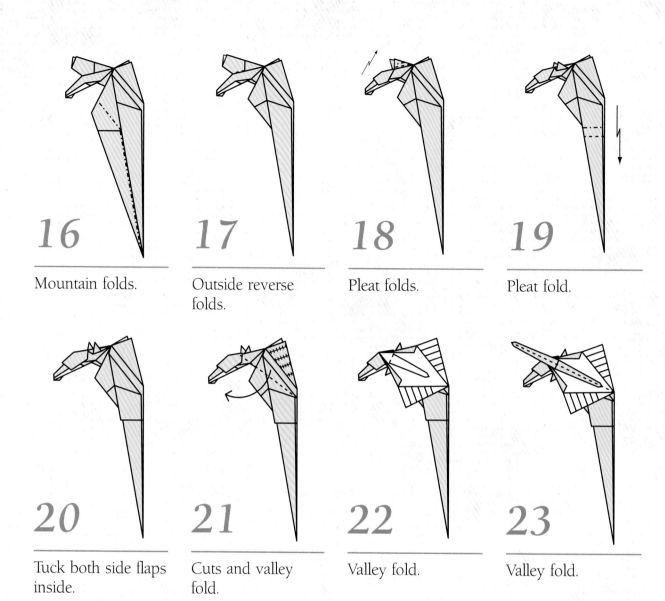

16
Mountain folds.

17
Outside reverse folds.

18
Pleat folds.

19
Pleat fold.

20
Tuck both side flaps inside.

21
Cuts and valley fold.

22
Valley fold.

23
Valley fold.

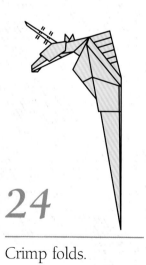

24
Crimp folds.

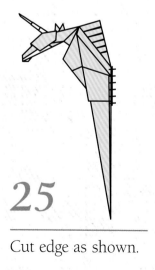

25
Cut edge as shown.

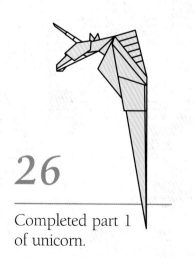

26
Completed part 1 of unicorn.

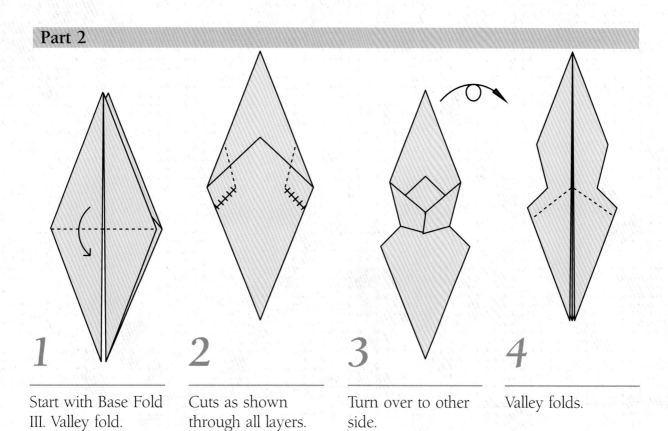

1
Start with Base Fold III. Valley fold.

2
Cuts as shown through all layers.

3
Turn over to other side.

4
Valley folds.

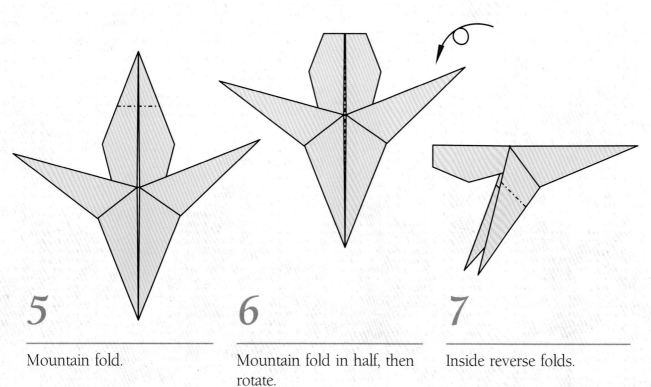

5
Mountain fold.

6
Mountain fold in half, then rotate.

7
Inside reverse folds.

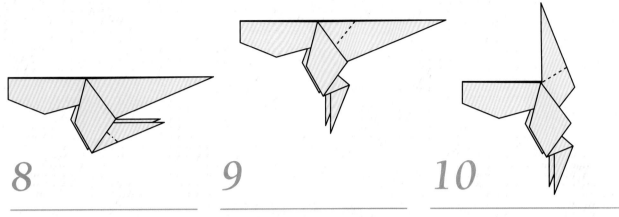

8

Inside reverse folds.

9

Inside reverse fold.

10

Repeat.

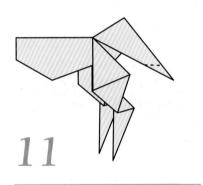

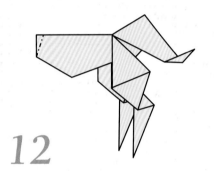

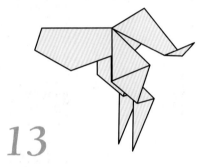

11

Outside reverse fold.

12

Inside reverse fold.

13

Completed part 2 of unicorn.

To Attach

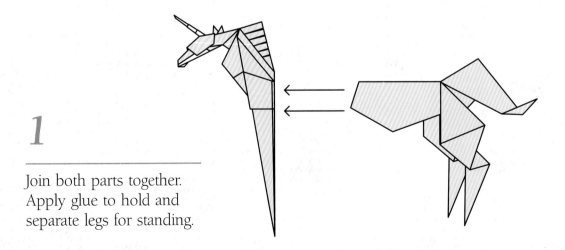

1

Join both parts together. Apply glue to hold and separate legs for standing.

Unicorn

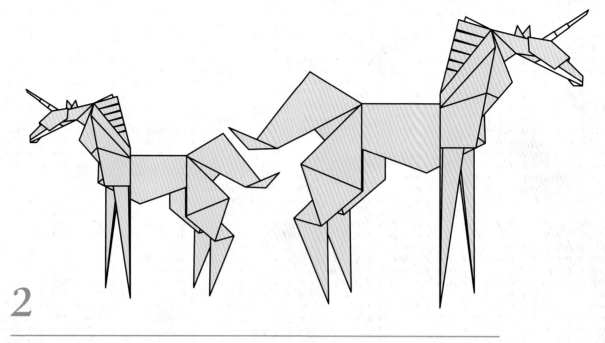

2

Completed Unicorn.

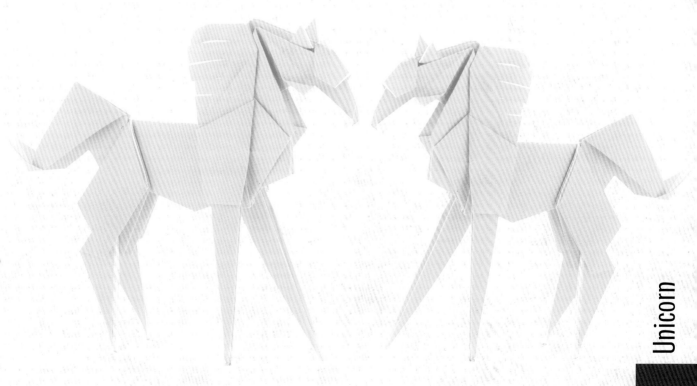

Medusa

Part 1

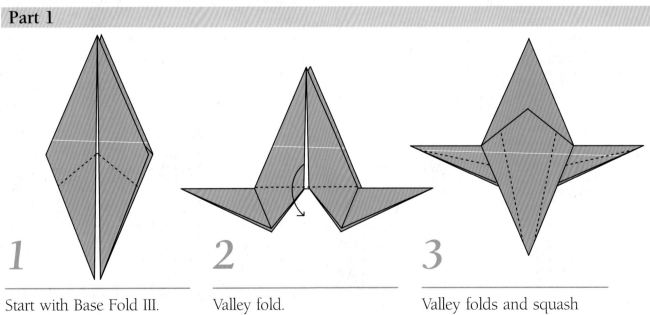

1

Start with Base Fold III.
Inside reverse folds.

2

Valley fold.

3

Valley folds and squash
fold.

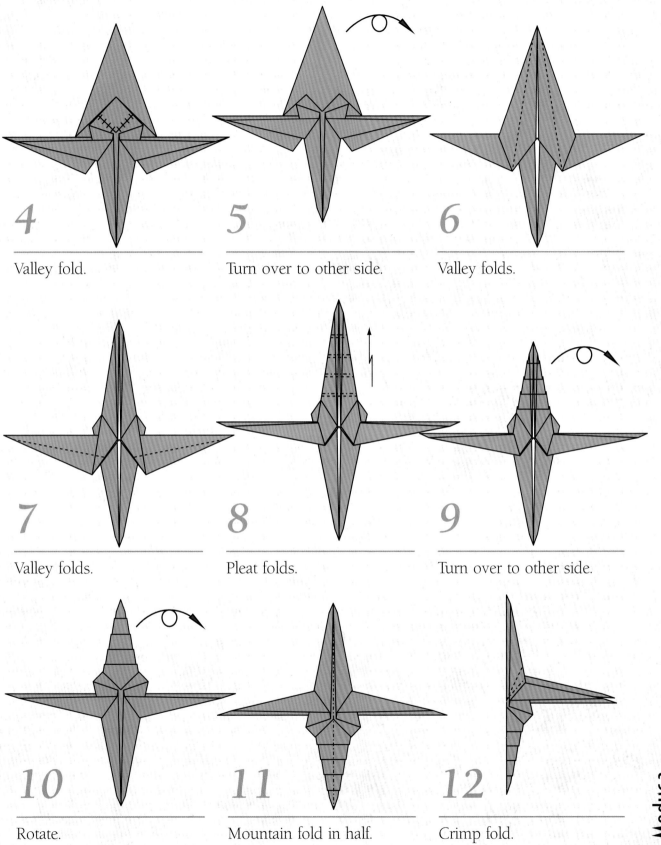

4

Valley fold.

5

Turn over to other side.

6

Valley folds.

7

Valley folds.

8

Pleat folds.

9

Turn over to other side.

10

Rotate.

11

Mountain fold in half.

12

Crimp fold.

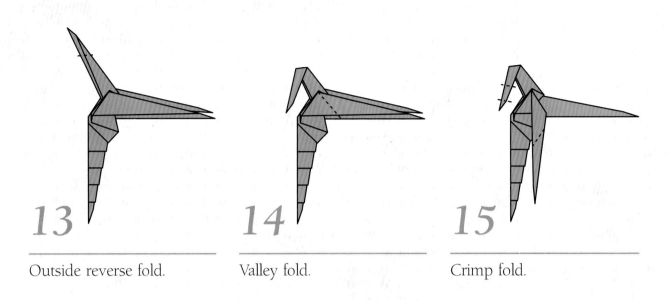

13
Outside reverse fold.

14
Valley fold.

15
Crimp fold.

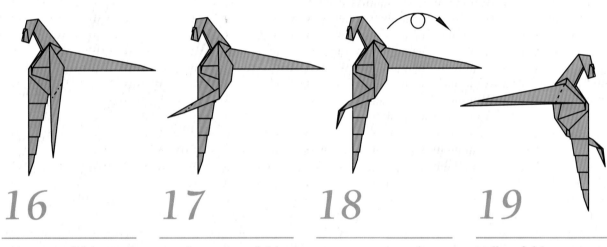

16
Mountain fold.

17
Inside reverse fold.

18
Turn over to other side.

19
Valley fold.

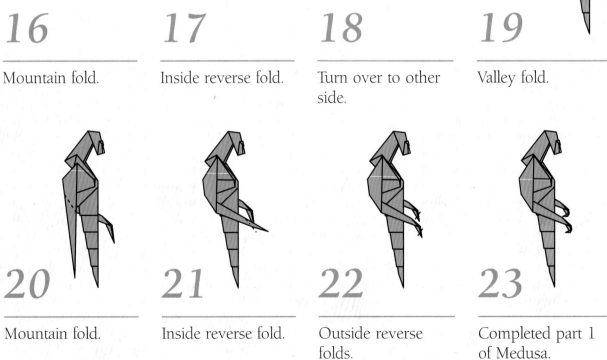

20
Mountain fold.

21
Inside reverse fold.

22
Outside reverse folds.

23
Completed part 1 of Medusa.

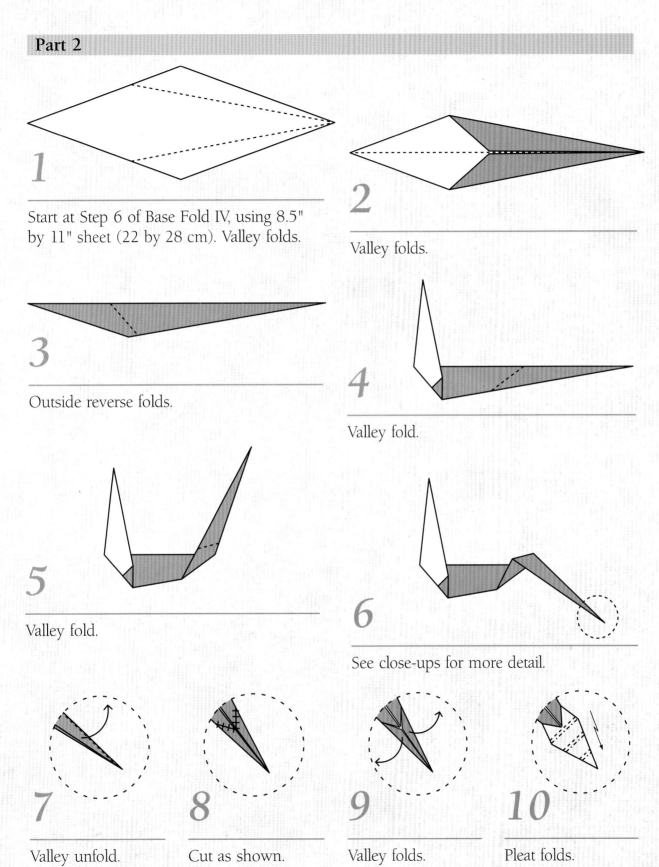

1

Start at Step 6 of Base Fold IV, using 8.5"
by 11" sheet (22 by 28 cm). Valley folds.

2

Valley folds.

3

Outside reverse folds.

4

Valley fold.

5

Valley fold.

6

See close-ups for more detail.

7

Valley unfold.

8

Cut as shown.

9

Valley folds.

10

Pleat folds.

Medusa

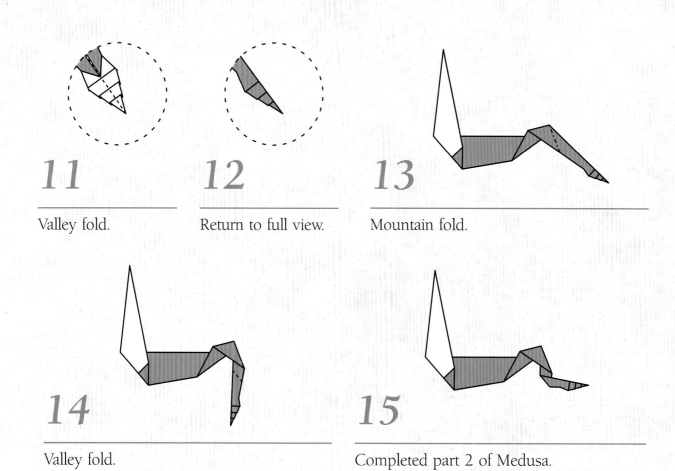

11
Valley fold.

12
Return to full view.

13
Mountain fold.

14
Valley fold.

15
Completed part 2 of Medusa.

Part 3 (hair)

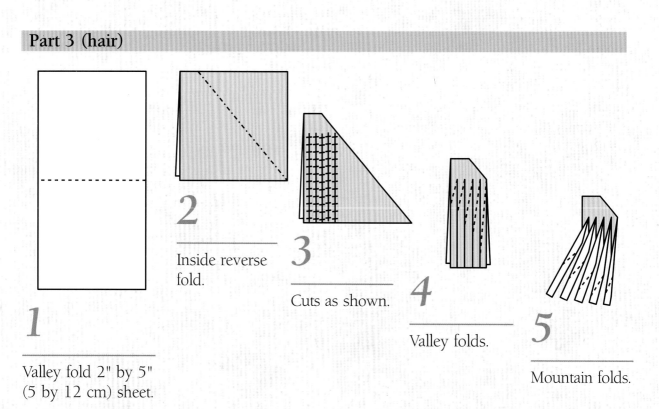

1
Valley fold 2" by 5"
(5 by 12 cm) sheet.

2
Inside reverse fold.

3
Cuts as shown.

4
Valley folds.

5
Mountain folds.

6

Valley folds. See close-ups for detail.

7

Pleat folds.

8

Trim "mouths." Back to full-view

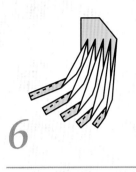

9

Completed part 3 of Medusa.

To Attach

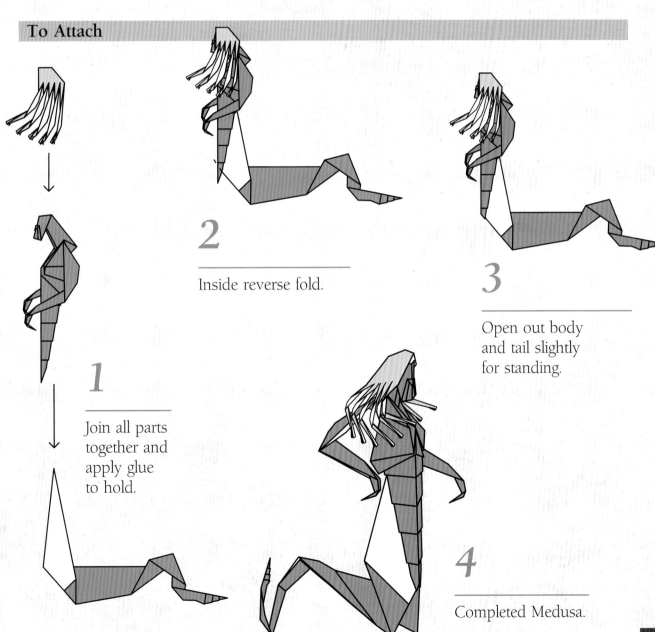

1

Join all parts together and apply glue to hold.

2

Inside reverse fold.

3

Open out body and tail slightly for standing.

4

Completed Medusa.

Medusa

49

Sphinx

Part 1

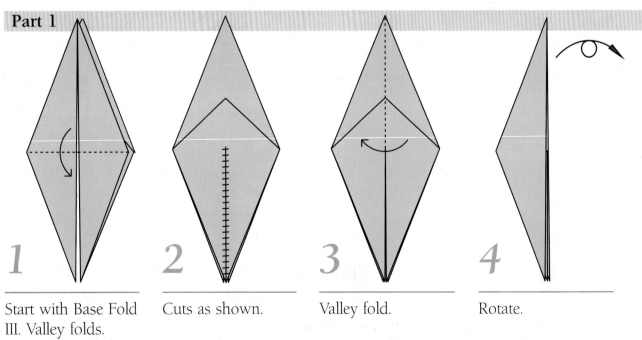

1

Start with Base Fold III. Valley folds.

2

Cuts as shown.

3

Valley fold.

4

Rotate.

Sphinx

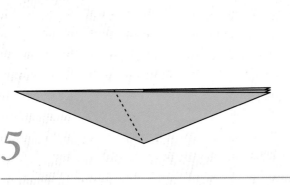

5

Outside reverse fold.

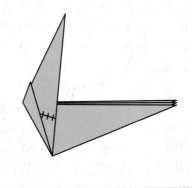

6

Make cuts to both sides.

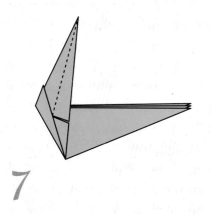

7

Valley fold both sides.

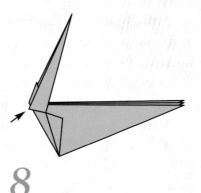

8

Tuck tips behind front layer.

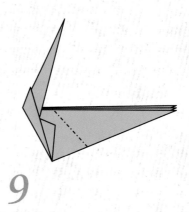

9

Inside reverse folds front and back.

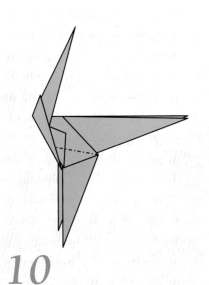

10

Mountain fold both sides.

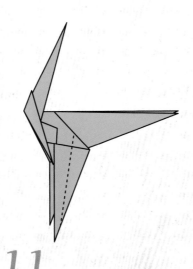

11

Valley fold both sides.

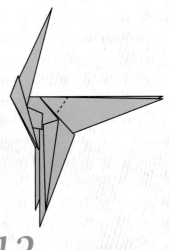

12

Repeat.

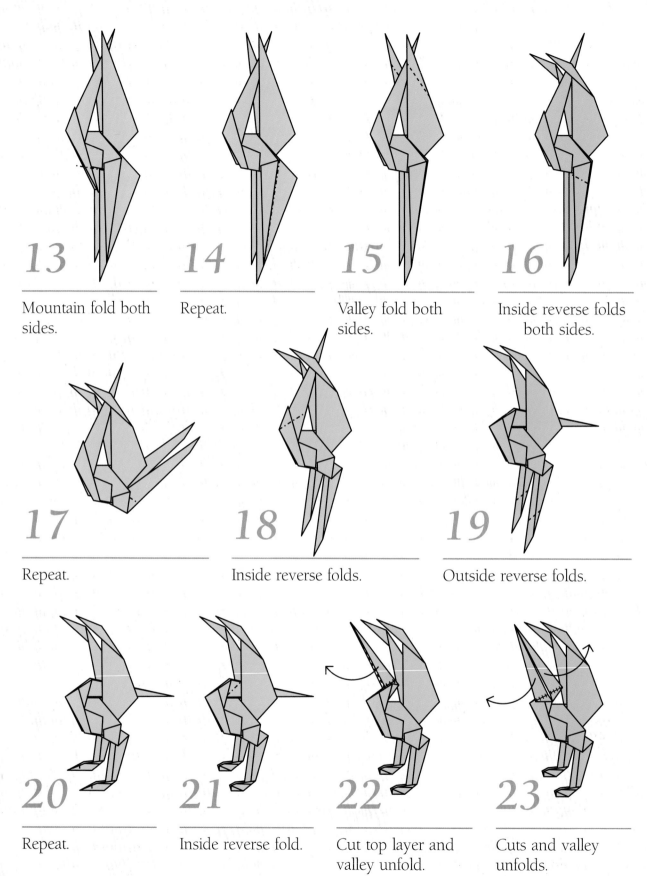

13
Mountain fold both sides.

14
Repeat.

15
Valley fold both sides.

16
Inside reverse folds both sides.

17
Repeat.

18
Inside reverse folds.

19
Outside reverse folds.

20
Repeat.

21
Inside reverse fold.

22
Cut top layer and valley unfold.

23
Cuts and valley unfolds.

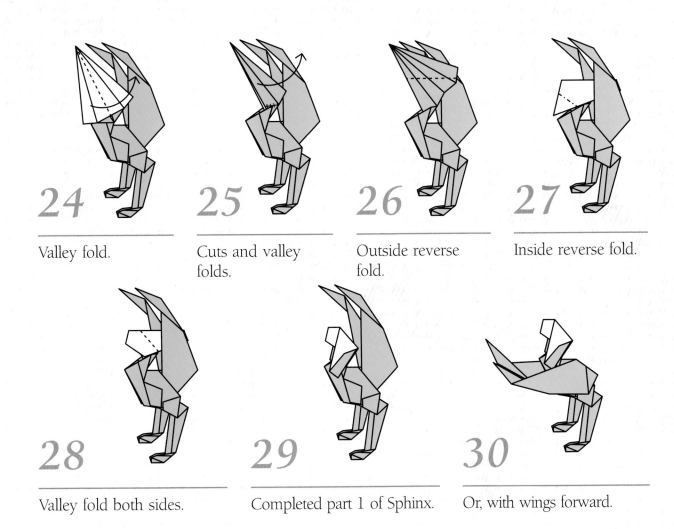

24
Valley fold.

25
Cuts and valley folds.

26
Outside reverse fold.

27
Inside reverse fold.

28
Valley fold both sides.

29
Completed part 1 of Sphinx.

30
Or, with wings forward.

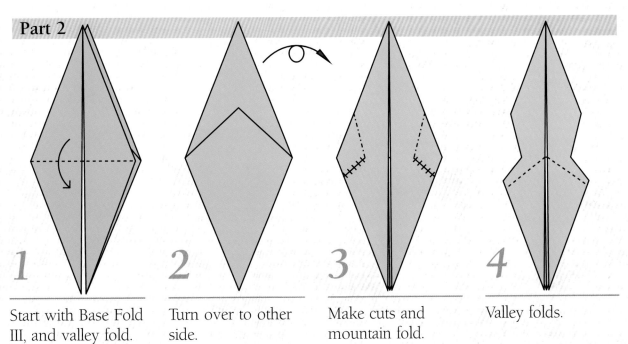

Part 2

1
Start with Base Fold III, and valley fold.

2
Turn over to other side.

3
Make cuts and mountain fold.

4
Valley folds.

Sphinx

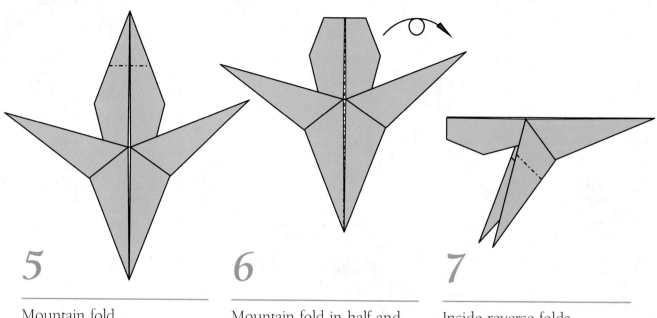

5

Mountain fold.

6

Mountain fold in half and rotate.

7

Inside reverse folds.

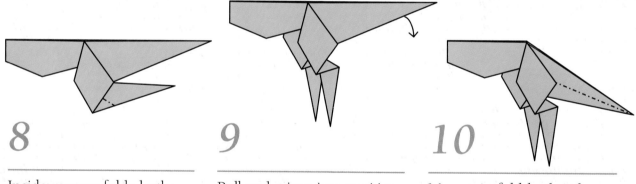

8

Inside reverse folds both sides.

9

Pull and crimp into position.

10

Mountain fold both sides.

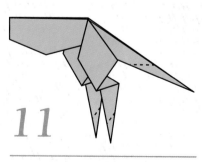
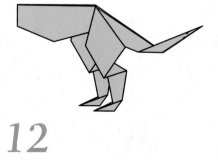

11

Outside reverse fold.

12

Inside reverse fold.

13

Valley unfolds.

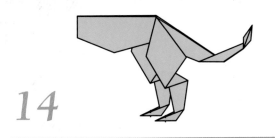

14

Outside reverse folds.

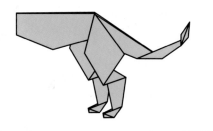

15

Completed part 2 of Sphinx.

To Attach

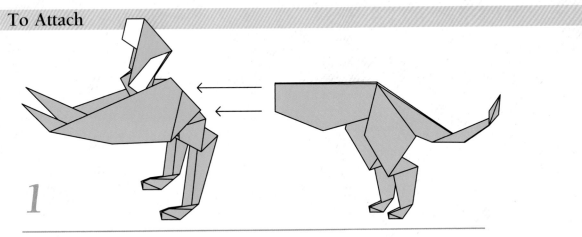

1

Join both parts together as shown and apply glue to hold.

2

Completed Sphinx.

Shiva Nataraja

Part 1

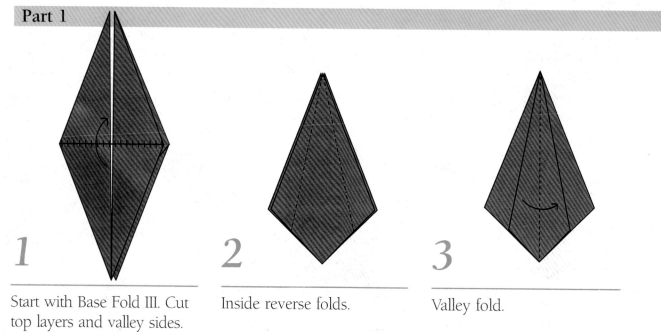

1

Start with Base Fold III. Cut top layers and valley sides.

2

Inside reverse folds.

3

Valley fold.

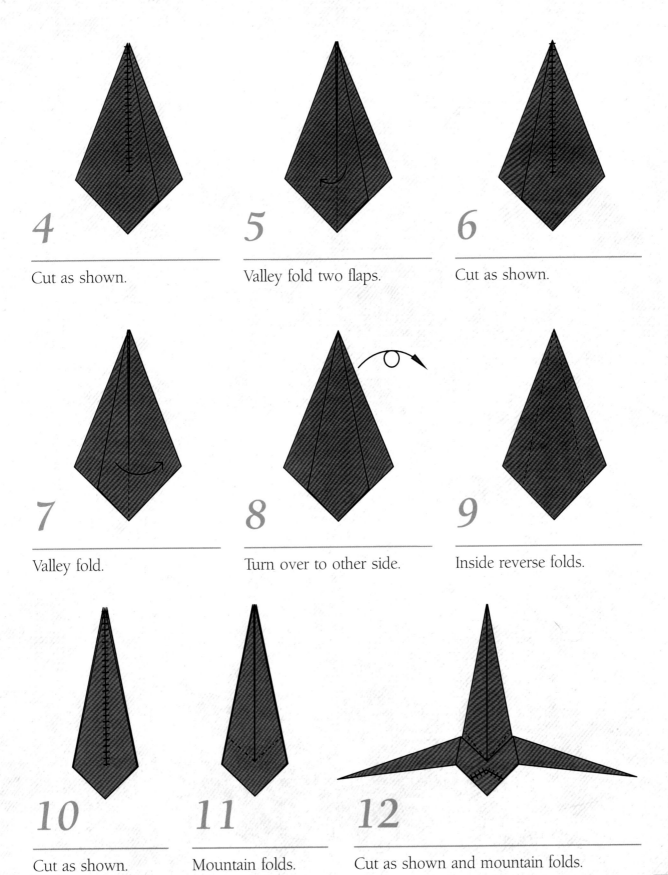

4

Cut as shown.

5

Valley fold two flaps.

6

Cut as shown.

7

Valley fold.

8

Turn over to other side.

9

Inside reverse folds.

10

Cut as shown.

11

Mountain folds.

12

Cut as shown and mountain folds.

Shiva Nataraja

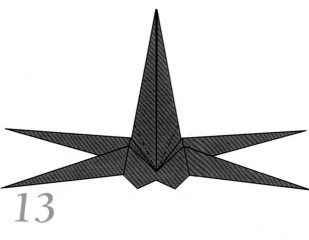

13

Mountain folds.

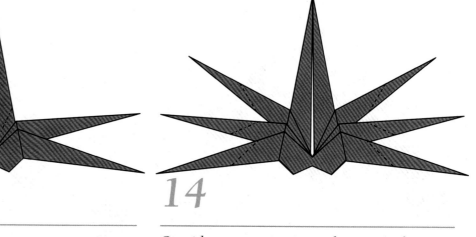

14

Outside reverse sections above. Inside reverse four others.

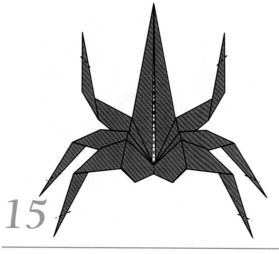

15

Repeat folds, then mountain fold in half.

16

Crimp fold.

17

Outside reverse top sections, inside reverse below.

18

Outside reverse fold.

19

Completed part 1 of Shiva Nataraja.

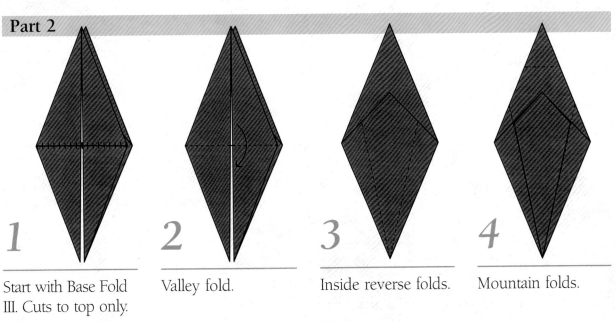

1

Start with Base Fold III. Cuts to top only.

2

Valley fold.

3

Inside reverse folds.

4

Mountain folds.

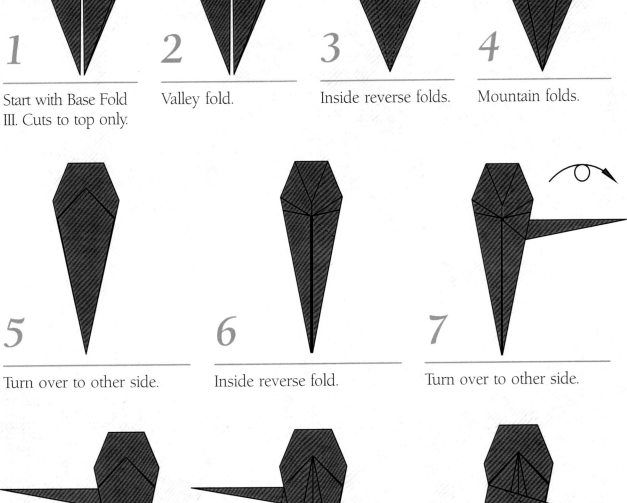

5

Turn over to other side.

6

Inside reverse fold.

7

Turn over to other side.

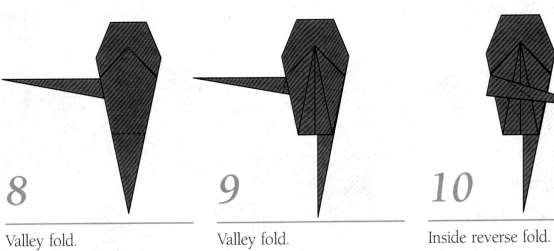

8

Valley fold.

9

Valley fold.

10

Inside reverse fold.

Shiva Nataraja

59

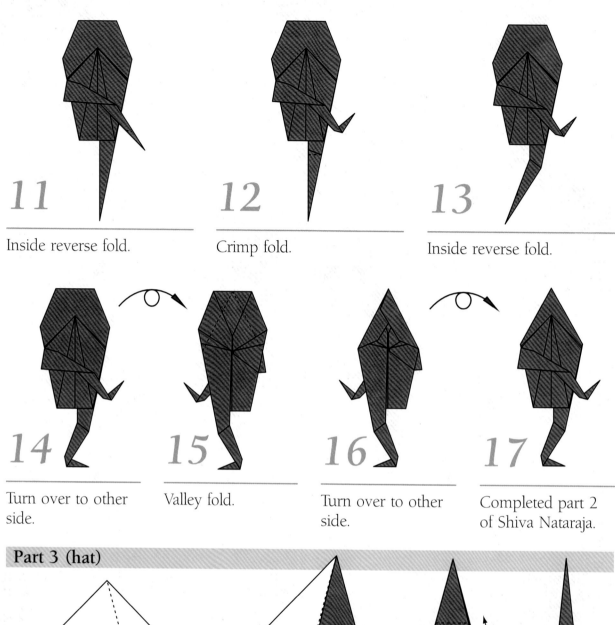

11

Inside reverse fold.

12

Crimp fold.

13

Inside reverse fold.

14

Turn over to other side.

15

Valley fold.

16

Turn over to other side.

17

Completed part 2 of Shiva Nataraja.

Part 3 (hat)

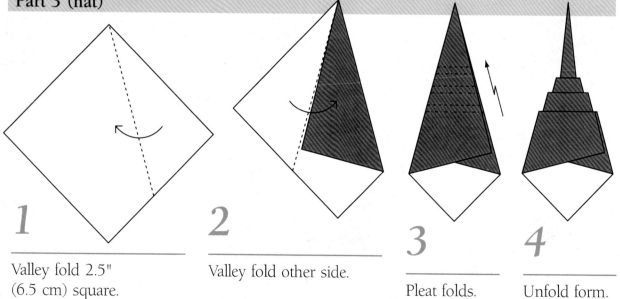

1

Valley fold 2.5" (6.5 cm) square.

2

Valley fold other side.

3

Pleat folds.

4

Unfold form.

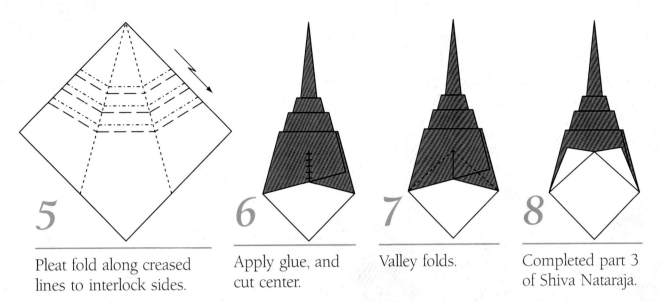

5

Pleat fold along creased lines to interlock sides.

6

Apply glue, and cut center.

7

Valley folds.

8

Completed part 3 of Shiva Nataraja.

To Attach

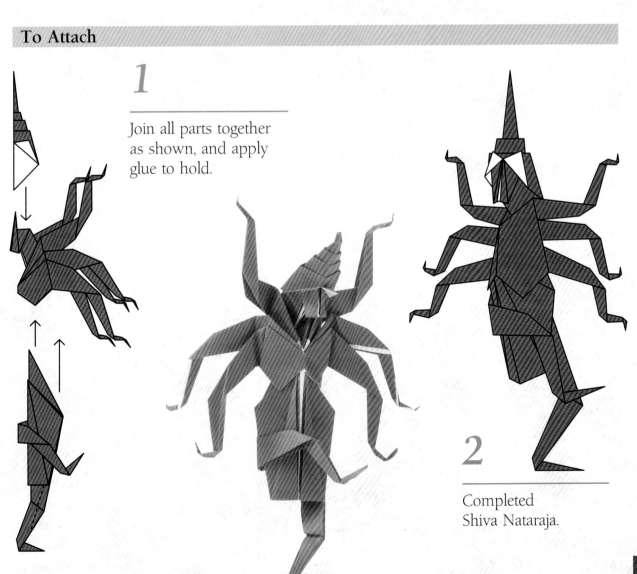

1

Join all parts together as shown, and apply glue to hold.

2

Completed Shiva Nataraja.

Standing Dragon

Part 1

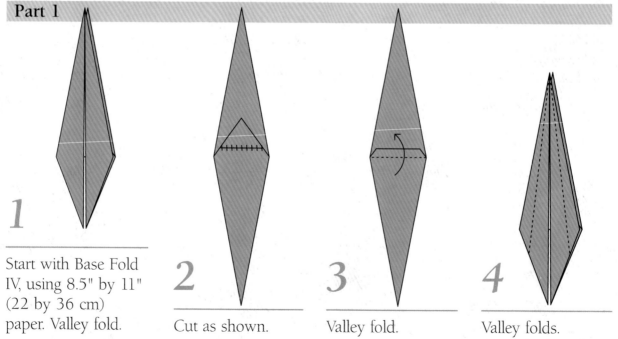

1

Start with Base Fold IV, using 8.5" by 11" (22 by 36 cm) paper. Valley fold.

2

Cut as shown.

3

Valley fold.

4

Valley folds.

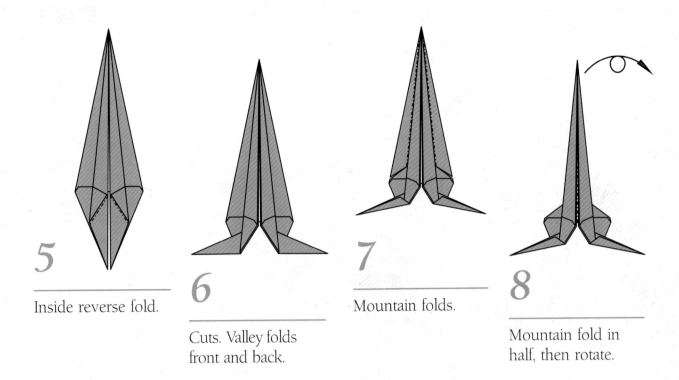

5

Inside reverse fold.

6

Cuts. Valley folds
front and back.

7

Mountain folds.

8

Mountain fold in
half, then rotate.

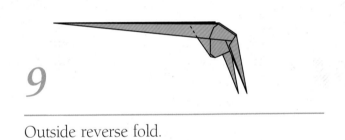

9

Outside reverse fold.

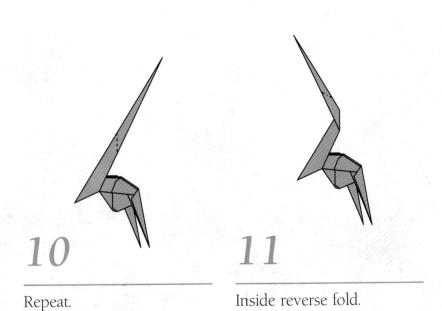

10

Repeat.

11

Inside reverse fold.

12

Unfold back to Step 8.

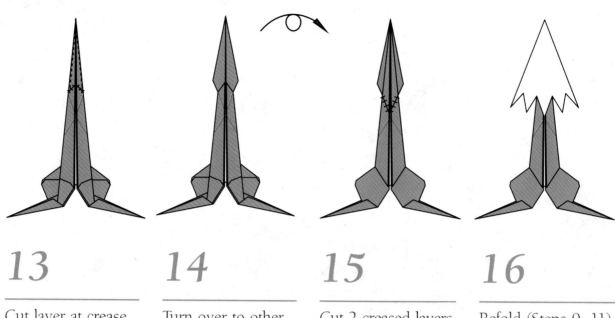

13

Cut layer at crease and valley unfold.

14

Turn over to other side.

15

Cut 2 creased layers only, and open out.

16

Refold (Steps 9–11).

17

Valley fold both sides.

18

Repeat.

19

Repeat.

20

Outside reverse fold.

21

Inside reverse fold.

22

Inside reverse fold.

Standing Dragon

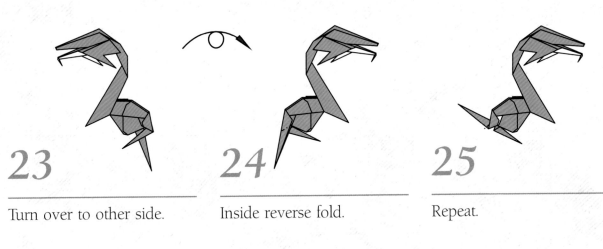

23
Turn over to other side.

24
Inside reverse fold.

25
Repeat.

26
Inside reverse folds.

27
Outside reverse folds.

28
Completed part 1 of standing dragon.

Part 2

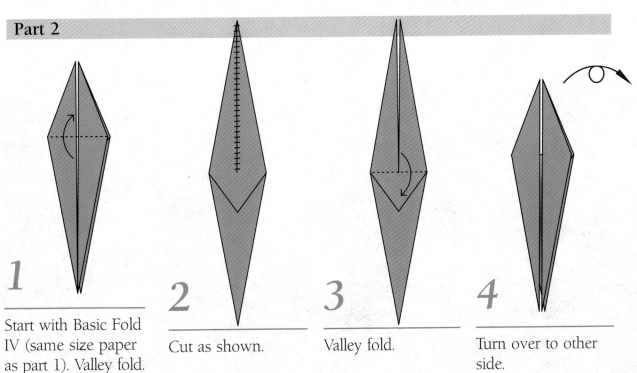

1
Start with Basic Fold IV (same size paper as part 1). Valley fold.

2
Cut as shown.

3
Valley fold.

4
Turn over to other side.

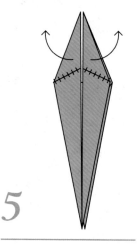

5

Cuts and valley unfold.

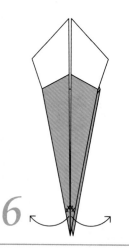

6

Repeat.

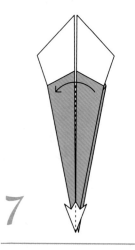

7

Valley fold in half.

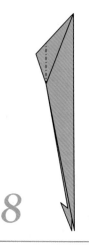

8

Mountain folds.

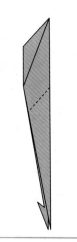

9

Valley fold.

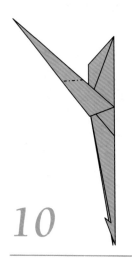

10

Mountain fold.

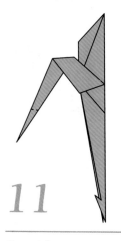

11

Outside reverse fold.

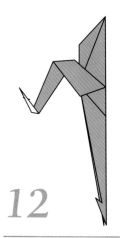

12

Repeat.

13

Valley fold.

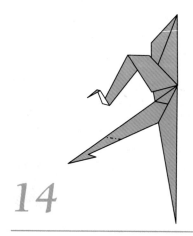

14

Mountain fold.

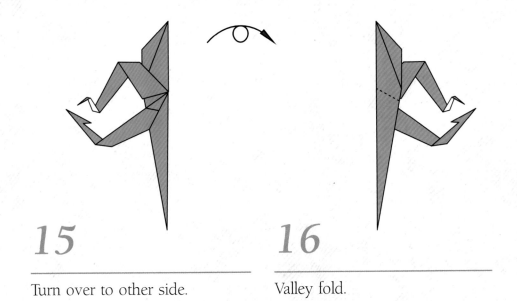

15
Turn over to other side.

16
Valley fold.

17
Mountain fold.

18
Outside reverse fold.

19
Repeat.

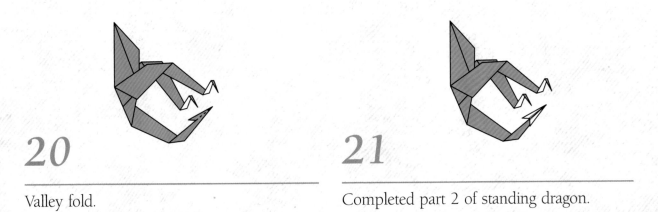

20
Valley fold.

21
Completed part 2 of standing dragon.

1

Start at Step 5 of Base Fold IV, using 4" by 10" (10 by 25 cm) sheet. Cut as shown, and rotate.

Right Wing   Left Wing

2

For each wing, valley fold.

3

Repeat.

4

Turn form over to other side.

5

Valley fold.

6

Open out wing.

7

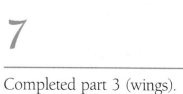

Completed part 3 (wings).

1

Crumple some brown or gray paper into a rock shape. Then join all parts together and apply glue to hold.

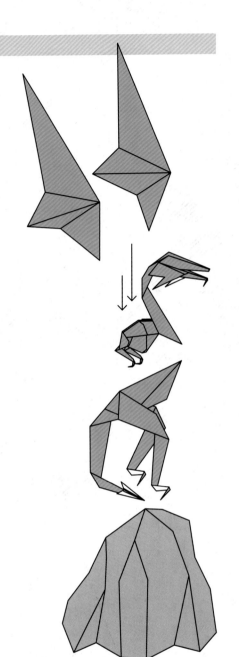

2

Completed Standing Dragon.

Centaur

Part 1

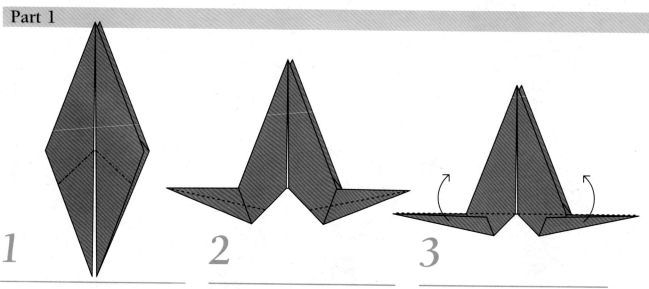

1

Start with Base Fold III.
Inside reverse folds.

2

Valley folds both sides.

3

Valley folds.

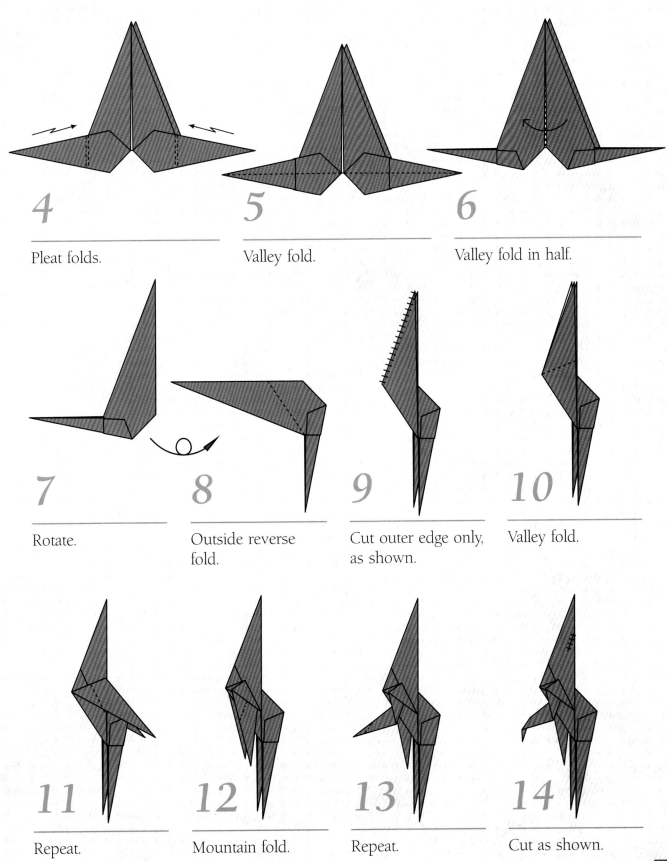

4

Pleat folds.

5

Valley fold.

6

Valley fold in half.

7

Rotate.

8

Outside reverse fold.

9

Cut outer edge only, as shown.

10

Valley fold.

11

Repeat.

12

Mountain fold.

13

Repeat.

14

Cut as shown.

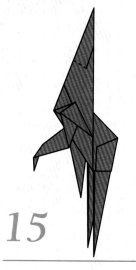

15

Outside reverse fold.

16

Repeat.

17

Repeat.

18

Inside reverse fold.

19

Cut and mountain fold. Repeat behind.

20

Turn over to other side.

21

Mountain fold.

22

Repeat.

23

Repeat.

24

Valley fold.

25

Pull and squash fold.

26

Completed part 1 of centaur.

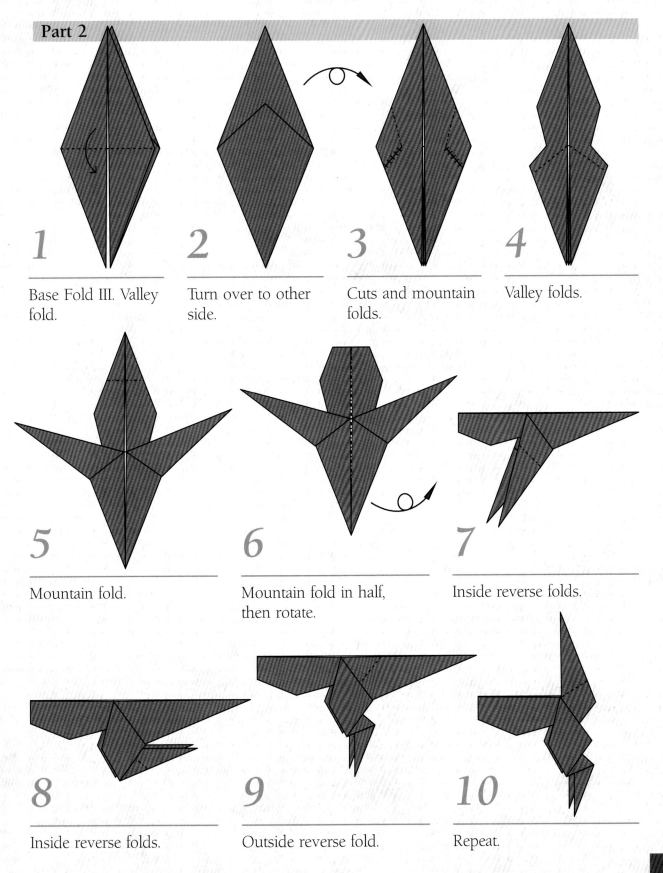

1 Base Fold III. Valley fold.

2 Turn over to other side.

3 Cuts and mountain folds.

4 Valley folds.

5 Mountain fold.

6 Mountain fold in half, then rotate.

7 Inside reverse folds.

8 Inside reverse folds.

9 Outside reverse fold.

10 Repeat.

Centaur

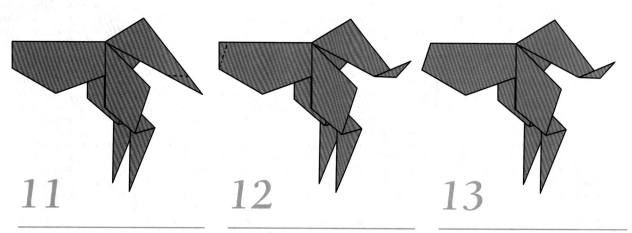

11
Outside reverse fold.

12
Inside reverse fold.

13
Complete part 2 of centaur.

Part 3 (headpiece)

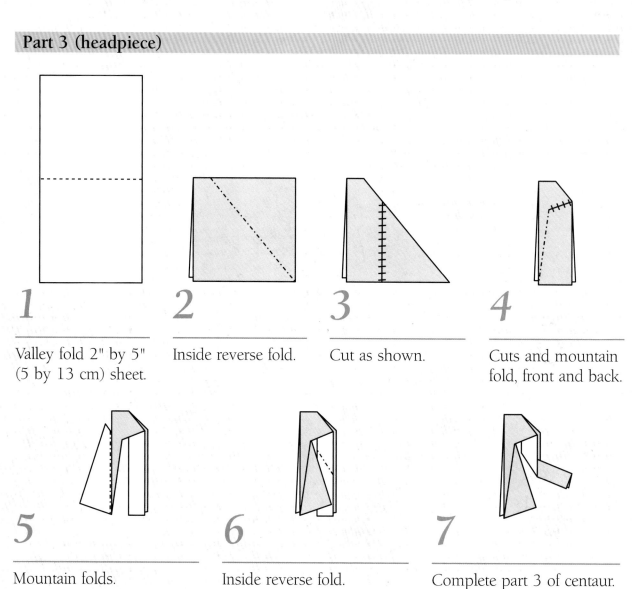

1
Valley fold 2" by 5" (5 by 13 cm) sheet.

2
Inside reverse fold.

3
Cut as shown.

4
Cuts and mountain fold, front and back.

5
Mountain folds.

6
Inside reverse fold.

7
Complete part 3 of centaur.

1

Join all parts together as shown. Apply glue to hold.

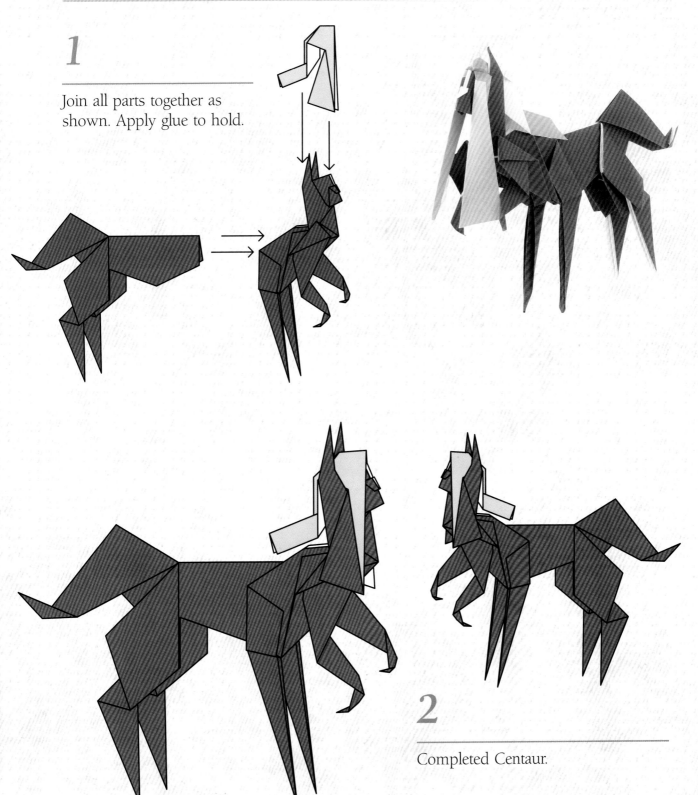

2

Completed Centaur.

Anubis

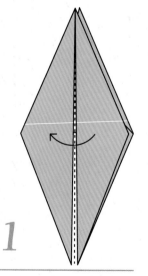

1

Base Fold III. Valley
fold front and back.

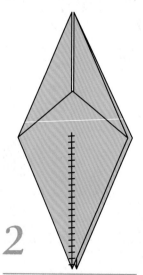

2

Cut as shown.
Repeat behind.

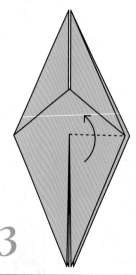

3

Valley fold and
repeat behind.

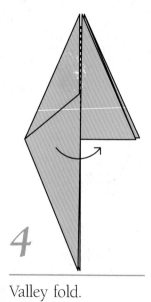

4

Valley fold.

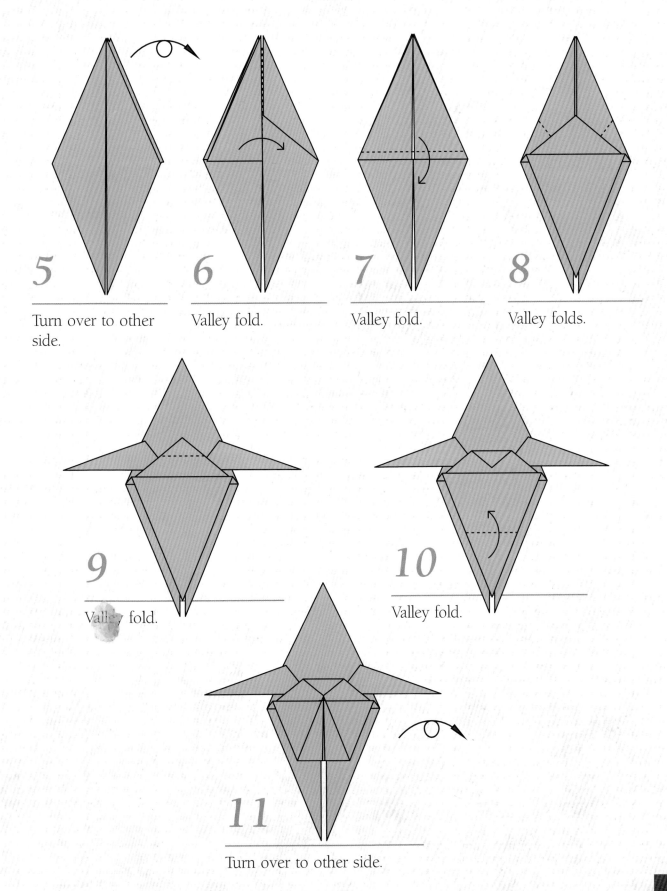

5

Turn over to other side.

6

Valley fold.

7

Valley fold.

8

Valley folds.

9

Valley fold.

10

Valley fold.

11

Turn over to other side.

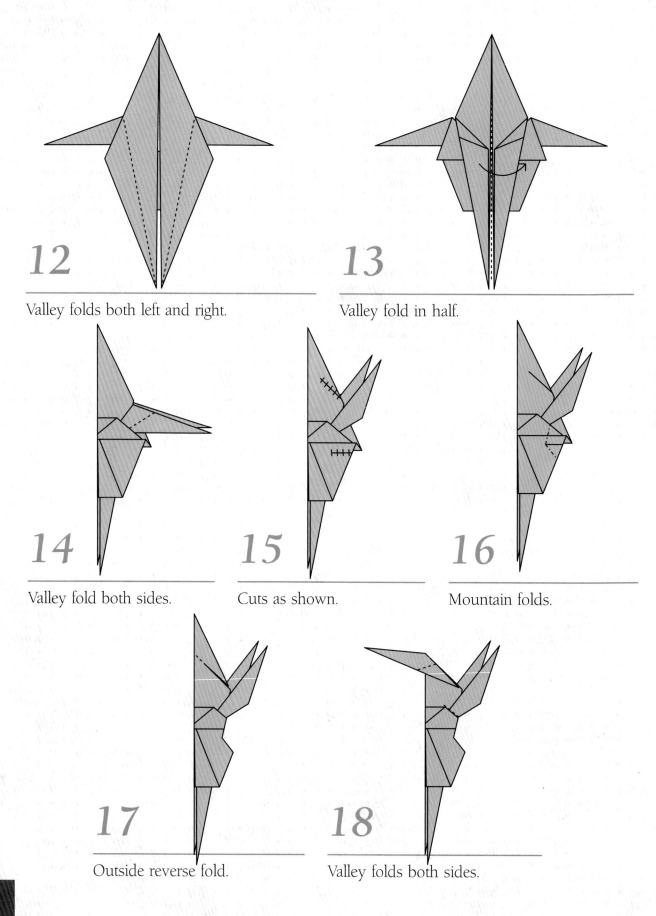

12

Valley folds both left and right.

13

Valley fold in half.

14

Valley fold both sides.

15

Cuts as shown.

16

Mountain folds.

17

Outside reverse fold.

18

Valley folds both sides.

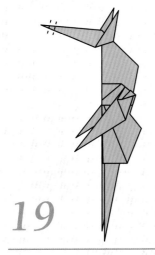

19

Outside reverse fold tip,
then repeat.

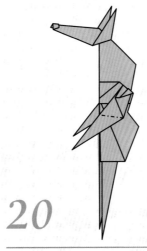

20

Mountain folds both sides.

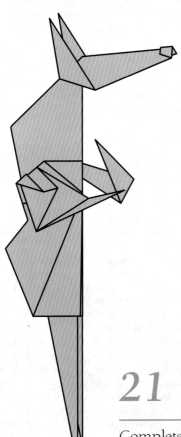

21

Completed Anubis.

Kraken

Part 1

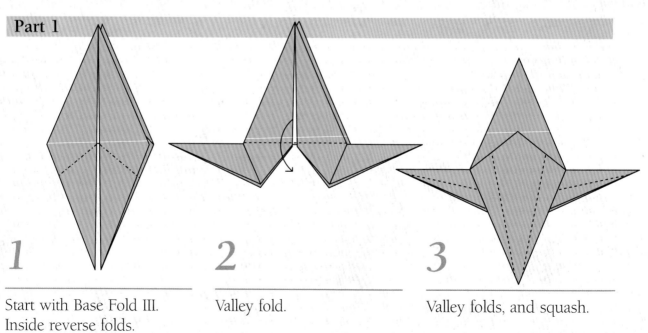

1
Start with Base Fold III.
Inside reverse folds.

2
Valley fold.

3
Valley folds, and squash.

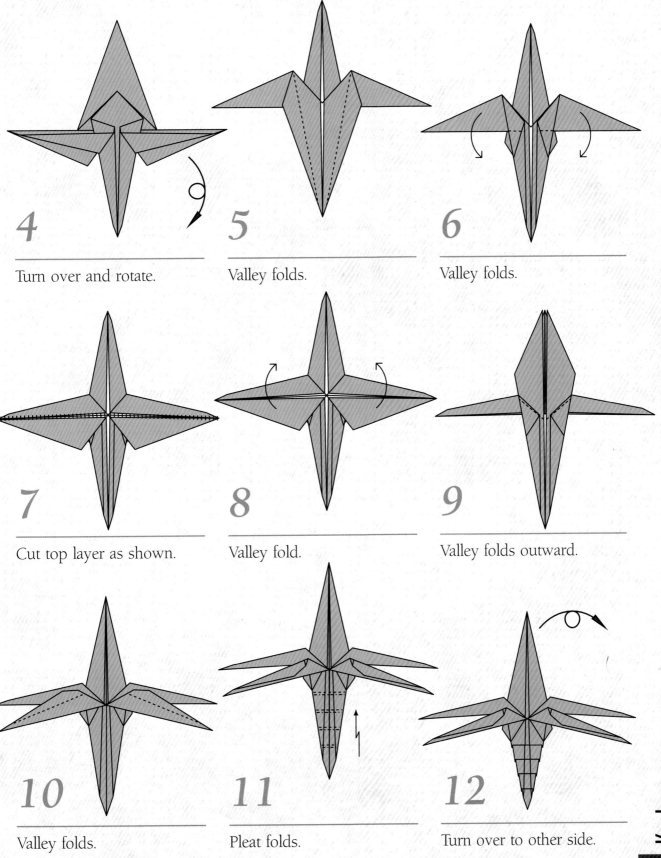

4

Turn over and rotate.

5

Valley folds.

6

Valley folds.

7

Cut top layer as shown.

8

Valley fold.

9

Valley folds outward.

10

Valley folds.

11

Pleat folds.

12

Turn over to other side.

Kraken

81

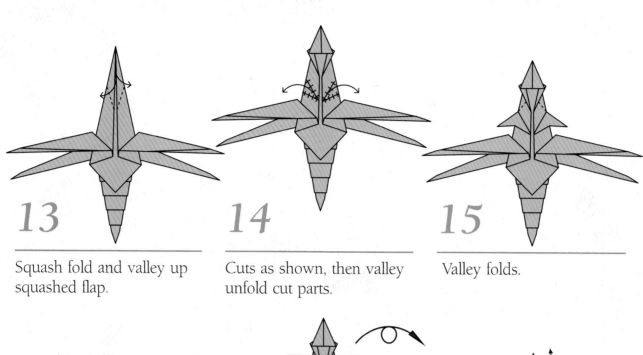

13

Squash fold and valley up squashed flap.

14

Cuts as shown, then valley unfold cut parts.

15

Valley folds.

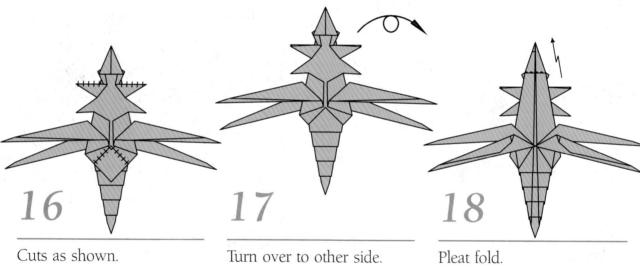

16

Cuts as shown.

17

Turn over to other side.

18

Pleat fold.

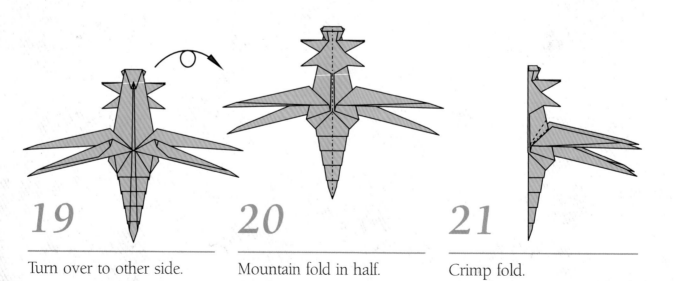

19

Turn over to other side.

20

Mountain fold in half.

21

Crimp fold.

Kraken

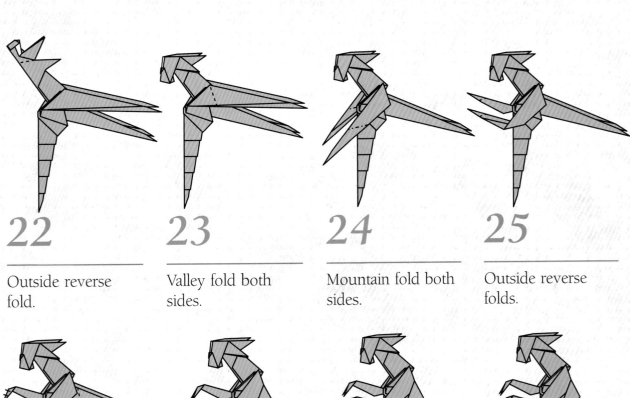

22
Outside reverse fold.

23
Valley fold both sides.

24
Mountain fold both sides.

25
Outside reverse folds.

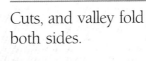
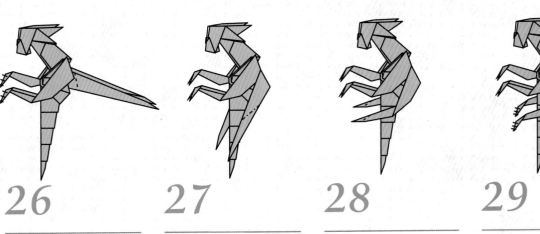

26
Cuts, and valley fold both sides.

27
Mountain folds.

28
Outside reverse folds.

29
Cuts as shown.

30
Mountain folds.

31
Mountain folds.

32
Pull to sides and valley crease.

33
Completed part 1 of Kraken.

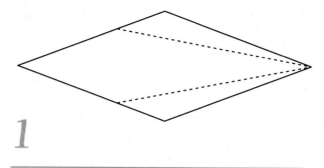

1

Start at Step 6 of Base Fold IV, using 5" by 11" (13 by 28 cm) sheet. Valley folds.

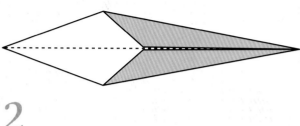

2

Valley folds.

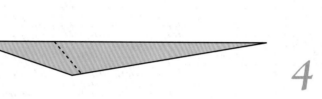

3

Outside reverse fold.

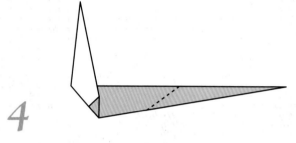

4

Valley fold.

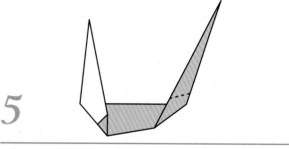

5

Repeat.

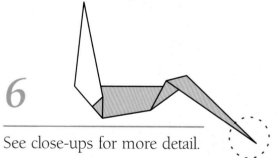

6

See close-ups for more detail.

7

Cut as shown and valley unfold.

8

Back to full view.

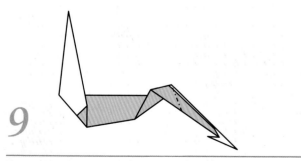

9

Mountain fold.

Kraken

84

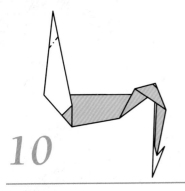

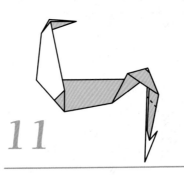

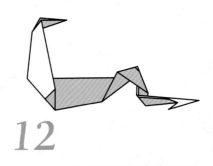

10

Inside reverse fold.

11

Valley fold.

12

Completed part 2 of Kraken.

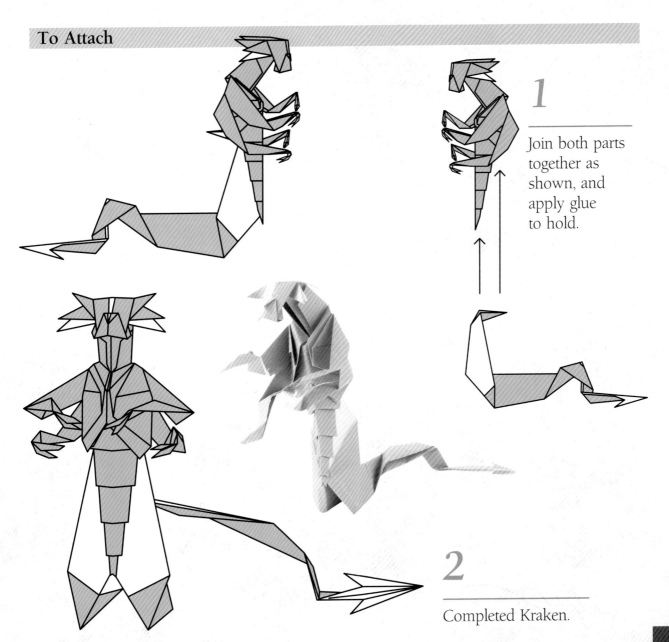

1

Join both parts together as shown, and apply glue to hold.

2

Completed Kraken.

Hydra

Part 1

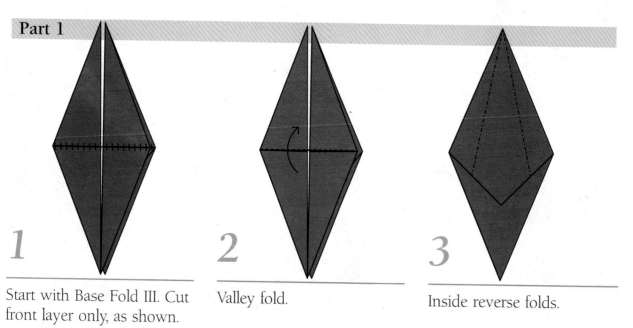

1

Start with Base Fold III. Cut front layer only, as shown.

2

Valley fold.

3

Inside reverse folds.

4

Cut as shown, then valley fold.

5

Cut and valley fold.

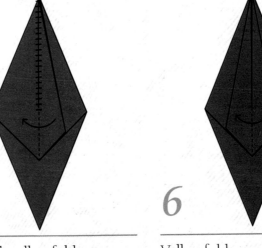

6

Valley fold.

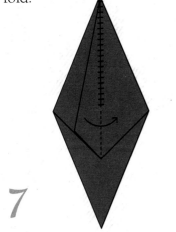

7

Cut and valley fold.

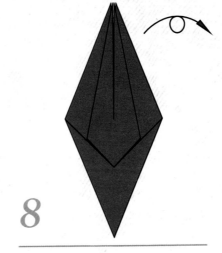

8

Turn over to other side.

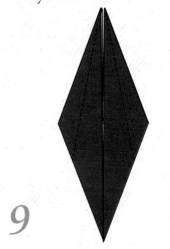

9

Valley folds.

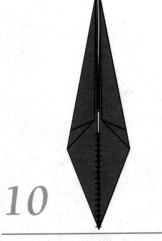

10

Cut as shown, front flap only.

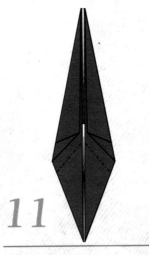

11

Mountain folds.

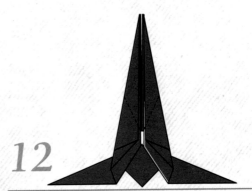

12

Mountain folds.

Hydra

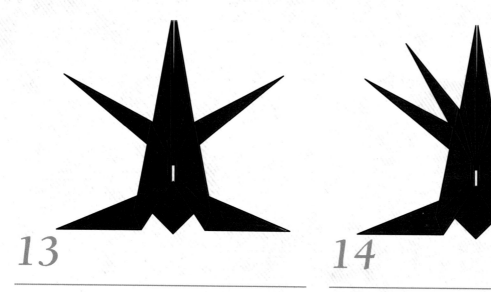

13

Mountain folds.

14

Mountain folds.

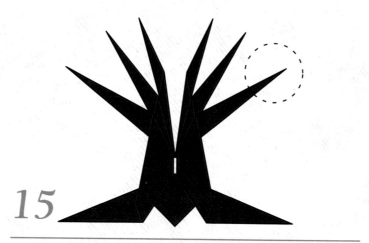

15

See close-ups for detail.

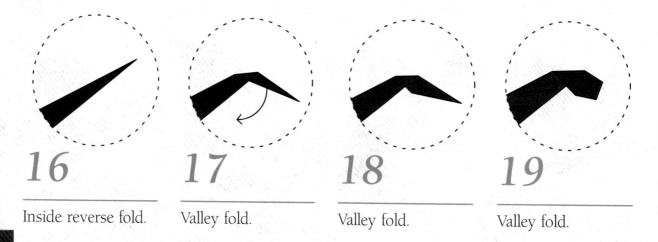

16

Inside reverse fold.

17

Valley fold.

18

Valley fold.

19

Valley fold.

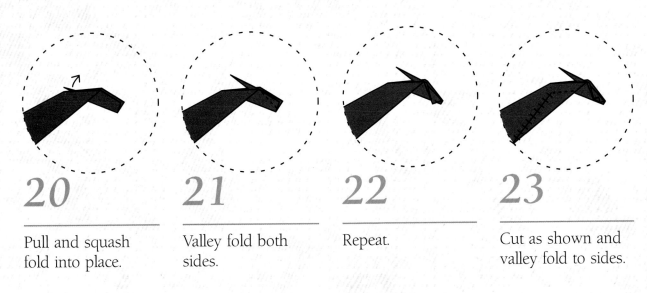

20
Pull and squash fold into place.

21
Valley fold both sides.

22
Repeat.

23
Cut as shown and valley fold to sides.

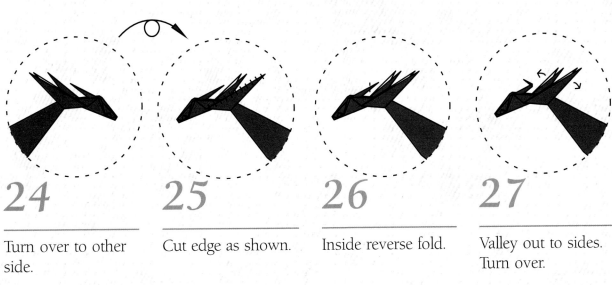

24
Turn over to other side.

25
Cut edge as shown.

26
Inside reverse fold.

27
Valley out to sides. Turn over.

28
Back to full view.

29
For other "heads," repeat Steps 16 through 28.

30

Outside reverse folds.

31

Repeat.

32

Repeat.

33

Inside reverse folds.

34

Mountain fold in half.

35

Completed part 1 of Hydra.

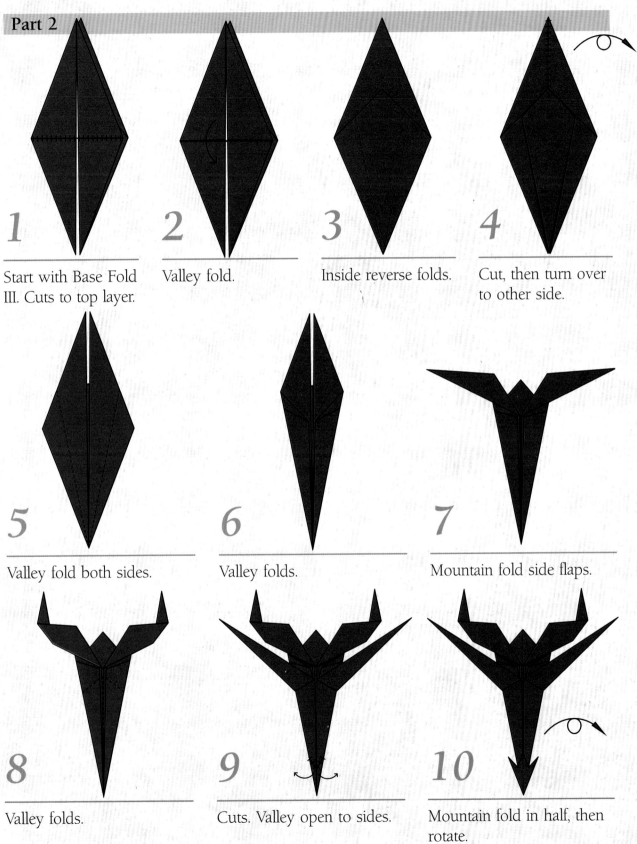

1

Start with Base Fold III. Cuts to top layer.

2

Valley fold.

3

Inside reverse folds.

4

Cut, then turn over to other side.

5

Valley fold both sides.

6

Valley folds.

7

Mountain fold side flaps.

8

Valley folds.

9

Cuts. Valley open to sides.

10

Mountain fold in half, then rotate.

Hydra

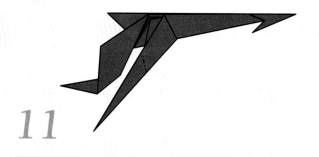

11

Inside reverse folds.

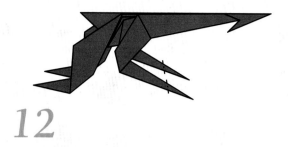

12

Repeat.

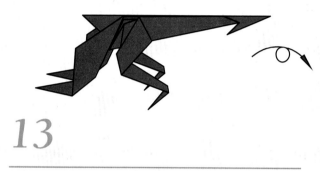

13

Rotate.

14

Pleat folds.

15

Pull and squash into place to add curve.

16

Completed part 2 of Hydra.

1

Join both parts together
and apply glue to hold.
Position heads, and open
out figure to stand.

2

Completed Hydra.

Denizens of the Hall

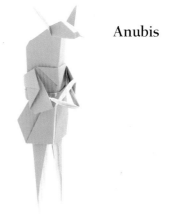
Anubis

Anubis In ancient Egypt, this jackal-headed god led the dead to judgment, weighing their hearts against a feather.

Centaur A horselike being with the upper body, head, and arms of a man.

Cerberus This huge 3-headed dog with a dragon's tail guards the entrance to the under-world so that none can escape.

Cyclops A giant being from Greek mythology, with a single eye in the middle of his forehead.

Flying Dragon This mythical serpent swoops with claws extended to snatch up prey.

Hydra A many-headed monster that grew two new heads whenever one was cut off.

Kraken A huge and horrific sea monster of Norse legend. With it's many long arms, it attacked sailing ships, drowning and eating the crew.

Medusa One of three hideous sisters with snakes for hair. Anyone looking at her was turned to stone.

Mermaid A shy sea creature with the head and upper body of a woman but the scaly tail of a fish instead of legs.

Shiva Nataraja This four-armed Hindu "Lord of the Dance" held in his hands the symbols of creation (a drum) and destruction (fire).

Sphinx Immortalized in stone in ancient Egypt, the winged Sphinx had the head of a woman and the body and tail of a lion.

Standing Dragon With wings extended, this scaly beast threatens all who come near.

Unicorn A horselike creature with a single long horn in the middle of its forehead.

Cerberus

Hydra

Sphinx

Shiva Nataraja

Centaur

Flying
Dragon

Hall of Myths & Legends

Kraken

Medusa

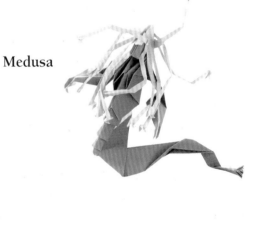

Mermaid

Unicorn

Cyclops

Standing Dragon

Index